OPERATION *ARCHERY*

The Commandos and the
Vaagso Raid 1941

KEN FORD

First published in Great Britain in 2011 by Osprey Publishing,
Midland House, West Way, Botley, Oxford, OX2 0PH, UK
44–02 23rd St, Suite 219, Long Island City, NY 11101, USA

E-mail: info@ospreypublishing.com

© 2011 Osprey Publishing Ltd.

A CIP catalogue record for this book is available from the British Library

Print ISBN: 978 1 84908 372 0
PDF e-book ISBN: 978 1 84908 373 7

Page layout by Bounford.com
Index by Alan Thatcher
Typeset in Sabon
Maps by Bounford.com
Originated by PPS Grasmere Ltd, Leeds, UK
Printed in China through Worldprint Ltd

11 12 13 14 15   10 9 8 7 6 5 4 3 2 1

Osprey Publishing is supporting the Woodland Trust, the UK's leading
woodland conservation charity, by funding the dedication of trees.

www.ospreypublishing.com

IMPERIAL WAR MUSEUM COLLECTIONS

Many of the photos in this book come from the Imperial War Museum's
huge collections which cover all aspects of conflict involving Britain and
the Commonwealth since the start of the twentieth century. These rich
resources are available online to search, browse and buy at
www.iwmcollections.org.uk. In addition to Collections Online, you can
visit the Visitor Rooms where you can explore over 8 million photographs,
thousands of hours of moving images, the largest sound archive of its kind
in the world, thousands of diaries and letters written by people in wartime,
and a huge reference library. To make an appointment, call (020) 7416 5320,
or e-mail mail@iwm.org.uk.

Imperial War Museum www.iwm.org.uk

AUTHOR'S NOTE

Throughout this book, I have used the Anglicized spellings of Norwegian
place names. All of the official reports on the raid used these spellings and
I have stuck with them for the sake of consistency. However, these place
names do not now reflect the present situation in Norway. For instance
what the British called South Vaagso is in fact the town of Måløy, with an
area of the town named Sor Vågøso (South Vaagso). For those interested in
the present names of the locations mentioned in the book, perhaps the
following English/Norwegian translations might be of interest: North
Vaagso/Nord Vågøso; South Vaagso/Sor Vågøso; Maaloy/Måløy;
Vaagsfjord/Vågsfjorden; Ulvesund/Ulvesundet; Rugsundo/Rugsundø;
Husevaag/Husevågøy and Hollevik/Holvika.

EDITOR'S NOTE

For ease of comparison between types, Imperial/American measurements
are used almost exclusively throughout this book. The following data will
help in converting the Imperial/American measurements to metric:

1 mile = 1.6km

1lb = 0.45kg

1yd = 0.9m

1ft = 0.3m

1in = 2.54cm/25.4mm

1gal = 4.5 liters

1 ton (US) = 0.9 tonnes

CONTENTS

INTRODUCTION

The depression and despondency that permeated the British nation after its forces had been evicted by the Nazis from mainland Europe in June 1940 did not last for long. The evacuation of the British Expeditionary Force (BEF) from Dunkirk had been the climax of a major defeat, but it was soon turned into something of a victory. A sense of relief spread through the country with the knowledge that more than 300,000 troops had escaped. There was also the realization that the nation and its empire were now on their own, answerable to no allies and in complete charge of their own destiny. A 'Dunkirk spirit' was born, and a new belligerent mood in the populace replaced the attitudes of the 'phoney war' that had stifled any offensive action. The appeasement-leaning mindset of the previous year or so was gone. Britain was determined it was not going to roll over and let the Germans walk in.

Prime Minister Winston Churchill's attitude towards Hitler echoed this mood; it was in his nature never to seek an accommodation with the Nazis. He saw the failure of British and French arms as the direct result of previous attempts by their governments to try to come to terms with the dictatorship and its global aspirations. In Churchill's view, there could be no peace until the monster that was German National Socialism was slain. Within days of the Dunkirk evacuation, Churchill sent a memorandum to his Chiefs of Staff asking how they might bring down 'a reign of terror' on German forces in the occupied territories: 'The defensive habit of mind which has ruined the French must not be allowed to ruin our initiative,' he ordered.

Churchill's memo struck a chord with LtCol Dudley Clarke, then Military Assistant to the Chief of the Imperial General Staff (CIGS), Gen Sir John Dill. Clarke had the idea of emulating the exploits of earlier historical irregular forces that had harassed and attacked their enemies at every opportunity. He reasoned that Britain should do the same, hitting the Germans across the Channel with lightning raids by amphibious guerrilla forces. He recalled that during the Boer War of 1899–1902, large numbers of British troops were tied down dealing with Boer irregulars. These *kommandos*, as they were called, were lightly armed raiders who would appear without warning, execute great destruction and then fade away. Might not the British now raise their own bands of *kommandos* to tie down and terrorize German troops? Clarke put the idea to the CIGS, who in turn raised the proposal with Churchill.

The project was exactly what Churchill was looking for, and permission was immediately given for Clarke to raise a group of men to carry out such raids at the earliest opportunity. It was a tall order, but fortunately some suitable troops were available in the shape of the Independent Companies that had been raised for the abortive Norwegian campaign of a few months earlier. These companies were composed of army volunteers who had been trained for light operations. Within three weeks, Clarke had planned and implemented the first cross-Channel attack of the war against German positions on the French coast near Boulogne. The raid accomplished little, for it was ill-planned and ill-equipped. Nonetheless, it did have a tremendous effect on the nation's morale. It showed that all was not lost. Britain was fighting back.

From this modest beginning the idea of raising a permanent special force dedicated to amphibious attacks against enemy shores was born. LtCol Clarke's *kommando* was anglicized into the English word 'commando', and

Lord Louis Mountbatten, Commander Combined Operations, inspects men of 3 Commando on board the transport ship HMS *Prince Leopold* in Scapa Flow prior to Operation *Archery*. (IWM, N504)

The naval commander for Operation *Archery*, R Adm Burrough, had his headquarters in the flag ship of the 10th Cruiser Squadron, the cruiser HMS *Kenya*. Co-located aboard the warship was Brig Haydon with his command post. The ship was chosen as the force headquarters for both land and naval operations to make best use of its excellent communication facilities. (IWM, FL9236)

the commandos as a unit were formed. The War Office authorized a Special Service Brigade to be created to raise a number of commandos and placed the formation under the control of the newly appointed Director of Combined Operations, Admiral of the Fleet Sir Roger Keyes. The admiral was a hero of World War I and had been the prime organizer of the classic amphibious raid on Zeebrugge in 1918. He was a great friend of Churchill and seemed just right for the job, but his forceful manner caused a good deal of friction with the chiefs of the other services.

The man chosen to lead the Special Service Brigade was Brig Joseph Charles Haydon. He was a regular officer from the Irish Guards who, before the conflict, had served as military assistant to the War Secretary, Leslie Hore-Belisha. Haydon had achieved some prominence a few months earlier in 1940, when he personally organized a special mission to the Netherlands to arrange for the escape of the Dutch royal family to England after the German invasion. Brig Haydon was now asked to oversee the raising of 11 army commandos. His organizational skills were put to good use when he began recruiting officers and men to form the new units. He started with those likely to be suitable as battalion commanders and left them to choose their junior officers and non-commissioned officers (NCOs) so that each of the commandos was populated with hand-picked volunteers. Haydon then used these lieutenant-colonels to help produce a training programme matched to the special skills required for amphibious raids. Brig Haydon continued to keep in close contact with each commando to ensure that every unit became proficient in its task of taking the fight back to the Germans.

ORIGINS OF THE RAID

By the summer of 1940, Germany had created a new map of Europe. A host of independent states had succumbed to a *Blitzkrieg* campaign by a disciplined and well-organized German Army. Modern warfare had arrived suddenly and unmercifully; the occupied nations found that their old order had been swept away, sometimes in just days, to be replaced by

Commando raids on German-occupied territories inevitably left much destruction behind. This was inflicted not only on German facilities, but also on the civilian infrastructure. When the raiders departed for home, they left towns and villages with just the wreckage of the factories that once gave them a livelihood. (IWM, 459)

**4 MARCH
1941**

**Operation
Claymore
carried out**

a new order under the control of a vengeful regime. The people of Poland, France, Belgium, Holland, Denmark and Norway now all had armies of occupation controlling their lives and there appeared to be little they could do about it.

Hitler then took steps to bring his new empire under his strict control. Nazi laws and edicts were implemented, draconian restrictions were placed on the local populations and their ability to take up arms against the invaders was removed, under pain of death. With most of Europe gradually being brought under the Nazi heel, there remained only Britain to be subdued. Few of the peoples of northern Europe believed anything other than it too would soon fall under the German yoke.

In 1940, German-occupied France did not need significant defences from outside attack – other than aircraft, Britain did not have the means to launch an assault. It was not until 1941, when Hitler turned his attention eastwards and invaded the USSR, that Germany needed to strengthen the defences of its Western territories. Up until then, it garrisoned its coastline with static newly formed formations using old positions built by previous regimes. Such improvisation made its forces susceptible to hit-and-run raids, and it was this weakness that the newly raised British commandos now looked to exploit.

The second British raid launched against occupied Europe took place in July 1940, before the commandos were actually formed. It was aimed at Guernsey in the Channel Islands, and was intended to bring back a few German prisoners for interrogation to find out information about the German garrison. The island had only been under occupation for a month and this raid was probably a little premature. It was hastily organized and chaotically executed, full of mishaps and mistakes: the boat crews were inexperienced; the landings took place on the wrong beaches; the intelligence was faulty; the troops were unable to perform their allotted tasks; the tides were wrong and the embarkation was a shambles. Nothing much was achieved, but the failure demonstrated that many new lessons had to be learned and implemented before further raiding parties could be unleashed against the enemy.

The results of the Boulogne and Guernsey raids showed Brig Haydon that his fledgling formation had to be trained and skilled if it was to mount effective attacks. Each commando needed to be brought up to an operational standard before it could be considered as being battle-ready. Suitable craft were required to carry the troops into action. New light weapons had to be designed. Men had to be hardened by rigorous and realistic exercises to achieve the necessary combat proficiency. They had to be self-reliant, independent, fit, able to march for long hours and capable of surviving in the open, relying on just their own initiative to stay alive. Organization and training now occupied the waking hours of all in the brigade.

Early in 1941, it was felt that a few of the new commandos were ready for action. Combined Operations Headquarters (COHQ) was by then looking at objectives for possible raids. Adm Keyes and his staff were trying to find likely targets that were suitable for amphibious operations. Churchill had been unimpressed with the previous year's Boulogne and Guernsey raids. He was no longer looking for pin-prick attacks to irritate the Germans; instead, he demanded punitive raids that would really hurt.

The war took an entirely new direction when Hitler invaded Russia in June 1941. Britain now had an ally in its struggle with Axis forces. As Hitler's army advanced eastwards, the Russians began asking for pressure to be applied to the Nazis in the West. All that Britain could realistically do, however, was to continue resisting the enemy in the Mediterranean and Middle East. Abortive actions were fought in Greece and in Crete trying to stem the pressure being applied by the Axis, and in North Africa the struggle against Rommel continued, but the Russians wanted more.

The Prime Minister asked Adm Keyes to launch more significant raids to help the Russians by tying down German troops in the West. In March 1941, Combined Operations came up with a prime target. The Lofoten Islands in northern Norway were the location of a number of fish oil factories and it was felt that a punitive raid on these targets would interfere with Germany's supplies and enable Combined Operations to test its effectiveness as a strike force. Nos 3 and 4 Commandos were chosen for the attack, each of them providing 250 men. In addition, 52 sappers were included for demolition tasks and 52 men from Free Norwegian forces would engage with the local population. Brig Haydon was in command of the expedition.

The attack on Vaagso and the earlier raid on the Lofoten Islands encouraged local civilians to leave for England to continue the war against Germany with the Free Norwegian forces. Many took up the offer, not just able-bodied men but whole families, including the elderly. Some Norwegians left after helping the raiders, fearful of German reprisals that could be aimed against them. (IWM, N497)

The raid, codenamed Operation *Claymore*, took place on 4 March. The troops landed at four different locations without opposition. They were warmly greeted by the local inhabitants, who sadly understood the need for the destruction of the factories and their main local industry. The commandos stayed for most of the day without any appreciable interference from the enemy. When it was time for them to leave, 315 Norwegians volunteered to go with them back to England. Ten quislings (Norwegian collaborators) were seized along with 225 of the enemy. There were no casualties. The raid tested the effectiveness of the Special Service Brigade and the work of Combined Operations, but failed to engage any of the enemy in combat.

The same was true for a raid on Spitzbergen in August 1941. Great stores of coal were set ablaze and a large number of Norwegian volunteers were brought back to Britain, but no real contact was made with enemy troops. The remainder of the summer of 1941 passed with a few cross-Channel raids by a number of commandos, all of which were hit-and-run attacks. Yet these raids were not tying down enemy soldiers, nor were they bringing any comfort to Russia. Combined Operations needed a big raid, one which would set alarm bells ringing in Berlin.

All of these raids required a great deal of cooperation from all three services (army, navy and air force), but this was not always forthcoming. Britain was in the throes of a great struggle and it would be several more years before it seemed likely that it could possibly win it. The Chiefs of Staff all knew that Germany could not be defeated until its armies were beaten in open battle. They were therefore reluctant to commit resources to raids and expeditions that, although good for morale and helpful for training, could be no more than a nuisance to the enemy. The army baulked at releasing some of its brightest young men for these ventures; the navy was becoming increasingly reluctant to commit warships that could be put to better use elsewhere, and the air force preferred to attack targets that would effectively reduce the strength of Germany's war effort. Adm Keyes found the task of trying to get the Chiefs of Staff to back his plans becoming more and more difficult, and his forceful and prickly personality did little to help his cause.

INITIAL STRATEGY

By October 1941, Adm Keyes' relations with the Chiefs of Staff had become so strained that Churchill decided he would have to be replaced as Director of Combined Operations. The Prime Minister had in mind a much younger figure, someone who could come up with bold and exciting schemes, and who would win over the Chiefs of Staff with a certain amount of personal charm and boundless enthusiasm. He chose a cousin of the King, Lord Louis Mountbatten, for the task.

Mountbatten was well known to the public through his widely reported celebrity lifestyle. A friend of politicians, film stars and royalty around the world, he had become one of the Royal Navy's most prominent figures. The 41-year-old Mountbatten had been a destroyer captain during the early part of the war and had lost his ship, HMS *Kelly*, in the Mediterranean in May 1941. He was then appointed as captain of the aircraft carrier HMS *Illustrious*. Mountbatten was in the United States whilst the ship was being refitted when the call came from Churchill for him to return to England.

There was some slight embarrassment in appointing Mountbatten as Director of Combined Operations, for with the rank of captain he was a rather junior officer. He now had to take his place on several of the Chiefs of Staff committees made up of the most senior officers in the land. To compensate, Mountbatten was promoted to commodore first class and a short time later was given the acting rank of vice-admiral when his title was changed to Chief of Combined Operations. He was also awarded an honorary commission in the army with the rank of lieutenant-general and in the RAF with the rank of air marshal. This was the first time that anyone other than the King had held rank in all three services.

With the arrival of Mountbatten at COHQ in London on 27 October 1941, there began a gradual acceleration of activity. With a younger and more diplomatic man in charge of Special Operations, one who was also a close relative of the King and a friend of the Prime Minister, relations with the planning staffs took on a more forceful and positive tone. Big raids now became priority, although Mountbatten announced that it was also his

R Adm Burrough,
Commander Naval Forces
for Operation *Archery*.
(IWM, A12770)

**27 OCTOBER
1941**

**Lord Mountbatten
appointed
Director of
Combined
Operations**

intention to launch at least one smaller raid every two weeks. The commandos were, at last, destined to see more and more meaningful action.

When Mountbatten arrived at COHQ in Richmond Terrace, London, he found that his planners were already looking for likely targets along the coastline of Europe, ones that might be suitable for commando operations. Mountbatten also wanted a location for a big raid, one that met the requirements laid out in an early memorandum on the subject. It had to be against a target that was within a mile of the sea with good landing beaches; one whose defences and garrison strength was known; and one that was clear of enemy concentration areas.

The planners at COHQ scoured the coastline from Norway to the Spanish border and compiled a list of possible targets for the big raid. One of the hundreds of sites identified was the small island of Vaagso in Norway, located on the North Sea coast to the north of Oslo. As a target it looked very promising: it was accessible from the sea, had a garrison of such size that it could be easily overcome and it contained industry that was vital to the German war effort. It was certainly one that was placed high on the list of potential objectives.

At the same time, another government department was also looking at Vaagso as a target. The Ministry of Economic Warfare was concerned with the vast quantities of fish oil that was being processed on the island and shipped off to Germany. It was considered vital that this trade was stopped or at least interfered with. The ministry had asked the Special Operations Executive (SOE) to look into ways of hampering this trade, and hoped that some clandestine operations could be mounted to sabotage the factories and put them out of commission. SOE had to decline such actions, for although the Norwegian resistance might well have been able to damage the plants, the inevitable German reprisals against the local population would be too great to warrant such an attack. The ministry turned to Combined Operations for help.

At first glance the importance of fish oil to any war effort might seem to be a little curious, but the substance was in fact of great value to the enemy. It was a remarkably rich source of Vitamin A, and was especially beneficial to German U-boat crews who would often go for weeks without seeing daylight. Deprived of the natural benefits of sunshine, submariners supplemented their diets with extracts of fish oil. The oil was also used to produce glycerol (glycerine), which was an essential ingredient in nitroglycerine used in the production of dynamite, gelignite and cordite. Fish oil was therefore an important strategic target and the destruction of any means of production was a useful and legitimate objective for Combined Operations.

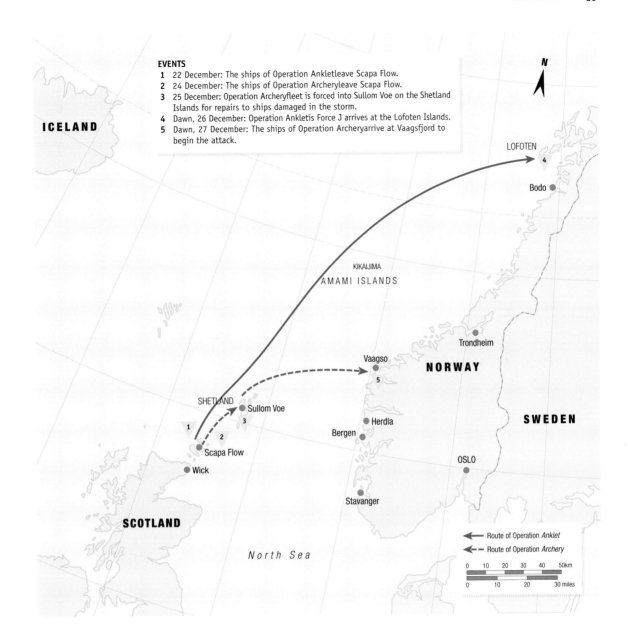

EVENTS
1   22 December: The ships of Operation Anklet leave Scapa Flow.
2   24 December: The ships of Operation Archery leave Scapa Flow.
3   25 December: Operation Archery fleet is forced into Sullom Voe on the Shetland Islands for repairs to ships damaged in the storm.
4   Dawn, 26 December: Operation Anklet's Force J arrives at the Lofoten Islands.
5   Dawn, 27 December: The ships of Operation Archery arrive at Vaagsfjord to begin the attack.

The news that the ministry wanted something done about the factories at Vaagso was enough to propel the island to the top of the file of possible targets. The more the planners looked into the site, the more they became convinced that this could be the objective they were seeking for the next great raid. Mountbatten was given a report on Vaagso and he concurred with the planners. With the commander of Combined Operations in favour, it was now time to try to get the Royal Navy and the Royal Air Force (RAF) on board to support the operation.

The island of Vaagso is situated off the western coast of Norway, facing out onto the northern edge of the North Sea. It is just one of thousands of islands that dot the rugged coastline, surrounded by a maze of inland waterways. Vaagso Island is located midway between Trondheim and

LtCol Durnford-Slater,
Commander 3 Commando.
(IWM, N406)

Bergen, around 220 miles north-west of the capital Oslo. The island is 7½ miles long by four miles wide and is separated from the mainland by a body of water known as the Ulvesund. It had, in 1941, a total population of around 2,500 people. The main town on the island is South Vaagso and it was here and in the nearby area that most of the fish oil factories were located, although the largest one of all was situated across the Ulvesund at Mortenes. Just a few hundred yards to the east is the small island of Maaloy. After the German invasion of Norway, a coastal defence battery was established at the southern end of the Maaloy Island to guard the channel into Ulvesund and the waterway of the Vaagsfjord, which led out into the open sea. South Vaagso and the island of Maaloy were identified by Combined Operations planners as the main targets for any proposed raid.

Holding the section of coast that included Vaagso was the German 181st Division, commanded by Generalmajor Kurt Woytasch. The division had arrived in Norway by air in April 1940 and took part in the campaign to capture the country. Since then it had been on garrison duties in the mid-western part of Norway. Allied intelligence suggested that area around South Vaagso would have a garrison of about 250 enemy troops from the division. More troops would be stationed on Maaloy Island along with the personnel from the naval coastal battery. To the north, on the western side of Ulvesund some six miles from South Vaagso, was another coastal battery at Halsoer. The battery defended the northern entrance to Ulvesund and hence faced to the north-east. This orientation would mean that its weapons could not be brought to bear on the landings to the south. The troops manning the defences could, however, be called upon to move south to oppose the landings, but it would take them some time to come into action. The approaches to the area off South Vaagso and Maaloy in the Vaagsfjord were covered by yet another battery positioned around 7km to the south-east, located high up on the island of Rugsundo.

Hitler had long felt that the occupation of Norway was vital to his war effort. The country was a source of war materials and a route through which Swedish iron ore was transported. After Hitler had taken possession of Norway in 1940, he proceeded to 'Nazify' the state to bring the country into line with his other conquered territories. He introduced an army of occupation and issued draconian dictates and orders to the general population. The moves triggered increasing opposition amongst the general populace. As the months passed, a vigorous Norwegian resistance movement began to emerge. Not surprisingly a certain percentage of the people took an opposite view and collaborated with the Germans, either because of ideological views, a desire for personal advancement, or simply a wish to live a peaceful life and be left alone. Prominent amongst this group was

Vidkum Quisling, a fascist Norwegian Army officer and politician. Quisling was appointed by the Nazis to serve as President of the collaborationist Norwegian government and cooperated in introducing the moves needed to bring the Norwegian people under German subjugation.

Just before Norway capitulated to the invaders in 1940 after two months of fighting, King Haakon VII escaped to Britain with members of his government. With the help of the British, he set up a Norwegian government-in-exile, and many of his countrymen who had escaped the occupation offered their services. Over the following years, many more people fled from Norway to join their exiled countrymen, and by the end of the war the number of Norwegian refugees abroad had grown to about 80,000. Of these, some 28,000 men and women enlisted in the services and fought for the Allied cause.

At the time of the invasion, many Norwegians were already in the service of their country as seamen. Norway had a sizeable merchant fleet of almost 1,000 ships, and a great proportion of these and more than 27,000 Norwegian sailors escaped to Britain and served alongside Allied merchant ships in vital convoys. The Royal Norwegian Navy also contributed 118 vessels for convoy escort duties and other operations. By the war's end, 58 of these were still in service. The Royal Norwegian Air Force (RNAF) was a relatively small service, able to provide aviators for just four active squadrons. The Norwegian Army contributed even fewer in numbers and received the lowest priority in equipment and support. Those troops that did see service mostly served in garrison, coastal artillery and hospital units. There were some notable exceptions, such as the Norwegian Independent

The Bristol Beaufighter was a long-range heavy fighter developed from the Beaufort torpedo-bomber, which was itself produced from the Blenheim light bomber. The Beaufighter was operational with the RAF during the war in almost every theatre. Although slow when compared to single-engine light fighters, its long range enabled it to provide air cover for Operation *Archery* from bases at Wick and Sumburgh in Scotland. (IWM, CH18583)

Company, No. 5 Troop of 10 Commando and a company set up to teach British troops the techniques required in winter warfare.

The earlier raid on the Lofoten Islands had enticed over 300 Norwegians to return to England with the assault force. The proposed raid on Vaagso was seen as another opportunity to allow many more Norwegians to leave the country and join Britain in the struggle against Germany. Provision was made to bring back as many people as possible during the raid, including whole families. Those who did not wish to leave would have to endure the inevitable savage German reaction to the landings. Before the operation, some thought was given to trying to ameliorate the damage and destruction that would be caused by the assault. It was suggested by Lord Mountbatten to the Chiefs of Staff Committee that sums of money should be taken on the operation for distribution amongst the inhabitants as compensation for any loss or inconvenience they might suffer, although he appreciated that there was a major point of principle involved in such a move. Gen Sir Alan Brooke was horrified. He said that the Chiefs of Staff could not agree to compensation being paid for damage that might be incurred during this or any other warlike operation, since it would establish an embarrassing precedent or might give rise to difficulties after the war. He was right of course, for Britain could not be expected to compensate countries for the damage that would be caused during the struggle to liberate the whole of

The destroyer HMS *Oribi*, part of the naval force for the Vaagso raid. HMS *Oribi* was an 'O' class fleet destroyer, and was launched in January 1941. It was armed with four single 4.7in guns, one quadruple quick-firing 2-pdr pom-pom, six single 20mm Oerlikon cannons and two quadruple 21in torpedo tubes. (IWM, FL17118)

Europe from the Nazi occupation. Although gifts of money would not be approved, the intention to take Christmas presents for the children of Vaagso remained as one of the more pleasant objectives of the raid.

Another interesting topic was raised at one of the Chiefs of Staff meetings. It was proposed to employ a smoke screen during the raid through which the commandos would be required to advance. It was suggested that it would be advantageous if they were allowed to wear civilian duty respirators. 'They could do without respirators,' the committee was told, 'but if the enemy put theirs on in the smoke, it would put the commandos at a slight disadvantage.' The Chiefs of Staff thought that the use of civilian respirators was not a good idea: 'There is the risk that the Germans, in seeing our troops emerge from the smoke wearing respirators, would assume that we were employing tocsin smoke and would accuse us of initiating chemical warfare. We could not incur this risk for the sake of a minor operation.' They had a good point.

One of the important aims of raiding enemy targets on mainland Europe was the opportunity to capture German documents and cipher machines. It was hoped that if surprise could be achieved during an attack, the enemy would have little time to destroy papers and other material that would be of great use to the Allied security services. Britain's ability to break German Ultra ciphered messages was unknown to Germany and virtually everyone in the UK. Just a few people at the very top, very few people indeed, knew

Free Norwegian soldiers accompanied all British raids on Norway, acting as interpreters and helping to capture known collaborators. They also took up arms against the Germans whenever they could. Here a proud Norwegian displays his country's flag, which he captured during his time ashore. (IWM, N461)

that some German coded messages were being cracked. The code-breakers at Bletchley Park were always eager to have new captured German Enigma coding machines, although these were understandably extremely difficult to obtain. The machines had a passing resemblance to a typewriter, and instructions in operational orders were given for all Allied officers to be on the lookout for them. Secrecy, however, had to be maintained, so a blanket request was made for a range of things to be collected from the enemy without singling out the Enigma machines specifically.

The following paragraph was included in instructions for dealing with captured vessels during the Vaagso raid:

> It is very important that ships, particularly escort ships, armed trawlers, etc, be prevented from destroying or throwing overboard any papers, etc. On boarding, a thorough search is to be made for papers especially those found in the charthouse, wheelhouse or captain's cabin. All papers are to be brought off and great care is to be taken to avoid damaging such documents or moving the keys of typewriters or similar machines as the value of their capture may be reduced thereby. The discovery of any of the above must be reported at once to the rear-admiral commanding 10th Cruiser Squadron. It is of the greatest importance that this signal should NOT be made in plain language.

The request to remove 'typewriters or similar machines' was a reference to the Enigma cipher machines, and the reference to avoid damaging or moving keys was very important to the cipher specialists at Bletchley Park. The actual position of the coding keys on the day of the attack would give the code-breakers an insight into the settings in use that day and perhaps, with information from other captured material, an indication of what the settings would be on other days.

PLANNING AND TRAINING

The German occupation of Norway caused many strategic headaches for Britain. Norway's long eastern coastline held many fjords and anchorages that were of great use to German shipping. The maze of islands that ran down the length of the coast provided sheltered routes for inshore German convoys, and shipments of iron ore could be made without recourse to voyages through open seas patrolled by the Royal Navy. From August 1941, the occupation was also a menace to the vital convoy routes carrying aid to

Training in Scotland included loading and launching assault landing craft from the troop transports. It was vital that each commando knew his correct position in his craft and was familiar with the process of embarking and disembarking from the tiny boats slung along the ship. (IWM, N470)

Russia. The threat posed by Hitler's capital ships was never far away from the sea lanes that led around the North Cape of Norway. The battleship *Bismarck* may have been sunk earlier in the year, but her sister ship *Tirpitz* was nearing a state of readiness and was poised to make sorties out into the North Atlantic and along the coast of Norway.

In addition to a raid on Vaagso, the Admiralty also wanted a show of strength in Norwegian waters to unsettle the Germans and demonstrate the effectiveness of British naval forces. They proposed a plan that would send a sizeable fleet of ships to the anchorages around the Lofoten Islands, with the intention of cutting German sea lanes and interfering with coastal traffic and shipments of iron ore. A large number of ground troops would also be landed to occupy a number of towns and villages and to set up a network of coastal guns and anti-aircraft sites – a figure of 3,500 was listed in one initial report. The islands were too far north to be reached by aircraft based in Scotland, so the force had to rely on its own defences against attacks by the Luftwaffe and German ground forces. The fleet was to occupy a sheltered anchorage, complete with tankers to refuel the warships during their stay. The naval vessels would then carry out sweeps to seek and destroy the enemy. It was expected that the force would remain at Lofoten for up to three weeks.

It was an ambitious plan, and one which rather alarmed the Commander-in-Chief (C-in-C) Home Fleet, Adm Sir John Tovey, who would be providing the ships. He was apprehensive about the time it would take to set up anti-

At the end of any operation, there were the inevitable souvenirs to be paraded. Here some of the raiders proudly display a captured Nazi flag after returning to their ship. (IWM, N527)

aircraft defences ashore. He felt that the Germans would react much more quickly to the operation than expected, and have aircraft over the landings in days rather than weeks. By that time they might well also have ground troops moving onto the islands. Adm Tovey suggested a slight scaling down of the operation by reducing the number of troops and relying on an increased amount of anti-aircraft protection, to be provided by the warships. He also reasoned that the high cliffs and mountains around the anchorage would themselves provide some protection from enemy air raids.

This smaller operation was approved by the Chiefs of Staff Committee, but the objective remained that this operation, codenamed *Anklet*, would have the same stated intentions as the previous plan. This was made clear by Admiral of the Fleet, Sir Dudley Pound: 'There is no question of altering the object of the operation – interruption of enemy sea lines of communication to Northern Norway, and in particular, the iron ore trade from Narvik.' He also thought that the stated time of three weeks duration could be reduced. Nonetheless, the intention was that the whole operation would not be an in-and-out raid, but a much longer occupation with the objective of upsetting the enemy and severing their coastal traffic.

The size of the fleet of vessels allocated to Operation *Anklet*, Force 'J', was impressive. One cruiser, four Fleet class destroyers, four Hunt class destroyers (two of which were Polish), two Norwegian corvettes, three minesweepers, one submarine, one survey ship, one ocean-going tug, two oil tankers, two assault troop ships and one Danish store and ammunition ship. The reduced landing force was to be provided by 12 Commando, some personnel from SOE (as observers) and men from the Free Norwegian 1st Brigade.

THE COMMANDERS

R Adm Harold Burrough, Operation *Archery* Naval Forces Commander

Born in 1888, R Adm Burrough had served in the Royal Navy since his midshipman days of 1904. In World War I he was gunnery officer in HMS *Southampton* during the battle of Jutland in 1917. At the outbreak of World War II, he was a staff officer in the Admiralty. He commanded the 10th Cruiser Squadron at the time of Operation *Archery* and had previously been engaged on the Arctic convoys to Russia. He later held command during the invasion of North Africa and in the Mediterranean and was eventually promoted to full admiral in September 1945.

Brig Joseph Charles Haydon, Operation *Archery* Military Forces Commander

Brig Haydon was a regular officer of the Irish Guards. At the outbreak of war he was serving as military assistant to the then War Secretary, Leslie Hore-Belisha. In 1940 he was among those who organized a special mission to bring the Dutch royal family out of the Netherlands after the German invasion. He was promoted to brigadier in 1940 and given the task of forming the commandos and organizing the raising of a number of battalions to undertake raiding operations. He was Military Forces commander on the early raid on the Lofoten Islands, Operation *Claymore*, and for the later raid on Vaagso. After Operation *Archery*, Haydon became Mountbatten's deputy at Combined Operations Headquarters. At the war's end, he was serving as a major-general.

Meanwhile, the plan for the Vaagso raid was finally agreed by Combined Operations, the Royal Navy and the RAF. It was then put before the Chiefs of Staff Committee for their approval before the undertaking could go ahead. No major operation could be mounted without first being screened by these heads of the three services to ensure that it fitted with the nation's overall strategic and manpower requirements. In mid November, permission was given for the raid. The navy were particularly in favour of it taking place, especially if it could be timed to coincide with Operation *Anklet*. This attack in southern Norway would act as a diversion for the larger operation in the north at Lofoten and split the Luftwaffe's response. Better still, Vaagso was within reach of RAF bases in Scotland, so that raid could go in with air cover, making it less likely that German planes could be moved northwards against *Anklet*. The Vaagso operation was given the green light under the codename *Archery*.

Operation *Archery* had a number of major objectives, the first and foremost of which was to destroy the fish oil factories in South Vaagso. Prior to this the main German gun battery on Maaloy had to be destroyed. Two other coastal gun batteries and a coastal torpedo station also had to be eliminated. The next objective was to engage and kill as many German troops as possible to take complete control of the town. Whilst clearing away the enemy, the local radio station was to be destroyed, all known Norwegian collaborators were to be rounded up and captured and as much intelligence as possible to be gathered from captured codes, ciphers and documents.

Once permission for the raid had been given, planning could begin in detail. With the backroom staff sorting out the fine details, the overall force commander and the individual commanders were chosen. Adm Tovey was appointed as the overall commander of the *Archery*/*Anklet* raids. For the raid on Vaagso, R Adm Harold Burrough was selected as the naval commander and Brig Joseph Charles Haydon chosen to lead the military forces (ground/amphibious forces) element of the landings. As the raid on Lofoten was primarily a naval operation, R Adm L. Hamilton was given the task of commanding both the naval and land aspects of the operation there.

R Adm Burrough was commander of the 10th Cruiser Squadron with his flag in one of the latest cruisers to join the fleet, HMS *Kenya*. His flagship was designated the headquarters vessel for the raid on Vaagso. As naval commander, Burrough had

One of the most famous of all commando weapons was the Fairbairn-Sykes fighting knife. Here a commando is being taught some of the finer arts of using the knife. It was designed to be a stabbing weapon, its long blade able to penetrate 3in of clothing before burying itself deep inside the body of one of the enemy. (Lt Gilbert A. Milne, Archives of Canada PA-183022)

responsibility for the deployment of the ships involved in the raid and for the bombardment of shore defences.

The date set for Operation *Archery* was 21 December 1941, although the force commanders were not named until 6 December. This left just over two weeks for the final plan to be worked out. Although the timescale was tight, most of the preliminary work had already been completed, and so it only remained for the commanders to finalize the fine details relative to their part in the operation.

The tasks to be carried out by the commandos ashore had already been clearly identified. Those men taking part in the attack had been training for months, repeatedly going over the principles and practice of amphibious landings. Each man knew his role in the enterprise, even though he did not know the actual target. The same was true for the naval contingent. For the seamen and their commanders, the attack on Vaagso was just another Combined Operations venture, so the final two weeks were occupied in the preparation of navigation plans, cruising timetables, bombardment tactics, escort duties and landing techniques.

Brig Haydon chose 3 Commando, led by LtCol John Durnford-Slater, to make the assault. Durnford-Slater had a unique claim to fame, for he was the very first British commando. When the call went out in 1940 for officers to join the fledgling formation, Durnford-Slater was the first man signed up by Brig Haydon. He was also given the command of the first commando unit

Assault landing craft in line ahead after being launched from their transport ship during an exercise in Scotland. (IWM, N469)

to be raised, 3 Commando, not 1 Commando as you might expect, for the titles of 1 and 2 Commandos had been allocated to the Royal Marines, who would raise these units some time later. Durnford-Slater took part in the initial commando raid of the war, when men from 3 Commando attempted their abortive attack on Guernsey in 1940. He had also led his men on the raid on the Lofoten Islands, along with parties from 4 Commando.

The number of tasks allocated to the commandos meant that Durnford-Slater had to supplement the strength of his commando with men from other units. Added to 3 Commando were a Royal Army Medical Corps (RAMC) detachment from 4 Commando, a Royal Engineer (RE) detachment from 6 Commando and two troops of commandos from the 1st Norwegian Independent Company (*Kompani Linge*). Also allocated to the attack were two troops (less one section) from 2 Commando. This latter group was to remain under the direct control of Brig Haydon as the floating reserve, ready to be put ashore wherever it was required during the battle.

The 1st Norwegian Independent Company was led by Capt Martin Linge. It was made up of Norwegians from all walks of life who had escaped to England. Some of them were from the area around the Lofoten Islands, and had taken the opportunity for a passage to England with the British troops during Operation *Claymore* earlier in 1941. Capt Linge had been in the country since April 1940 and was one of the first of the Norwegian ex-patriates to arrive. He had been wounded in the fighting that followed the German invasion of Norway and had been evacuated in a hospital ship to England.

After the Germans had captured Norway, they brought with them and used many weapons that they had seized from other countries they had conquered. They also used old and obsolete guns of their own, putting them to good use in coastal batteries and at other strategic positions. The battery on Maaloy Island consisted of German 10.5cm light field howitzers of World War I vintage. (IWM, N464)

Linge was screened by the Secret Service to ensure that he was not a German 'plant', and was asked to form a military unit from other Norwegians who arrived in the country. He was based in the Norwegian Embassy at Kingston House in London, along with the Norwegian government-in-exile. The group was under the control of the SOE and originally trained for clandestine operations in Norway such as sabotage attacks, organizing underground resistance networks and gathering intelligence. These men undertook the same training as those in the Special Service Brigade, and became the equivalent of British commandos. This professionalism made their presence vital in any Norwegian raid, for they were able to liaise with civilians, round up collaborators and also fight alongside the British commandos as equals.

R Adm Burrough's naval force comprised warships selected for special tasks. All had the overall protection of the amphibious force as their main concern, but each had other particular roles. HMS *Kenya*, with its 12 6in guns, was the main bombardment vessel, chosen to take on the German gun batteries around Vaagso with its overwhelming firepower. It was also the headquarters ship for the operation, and would be the communications

FORCES TAKING PART IN OPERATION *ARCHERY*

Naval Forces
HMS *Kenya* – Fiji class cruiser
HMS *Onslow* – 'O' class destroyer
HMS *Oribi* – 'O' class destroyer
HMS *Offa* – 'O' class destroyer
HMS *Chiddingfold* – Type II Hunt class destroyer
HMS *Prince Charles* – Assault troop transporter
HMS *Prince Leopold* – Assault troop transporter
HMS *Tuna* – 'T' class submarine

Military Forces
Operational HQ Special Service Brigade
Special Service Brigade Signal Section
3 Commando
Two troops of 2 Commando
RAMC Detachment from 4 Commando
Company from Free Norwegian 1st Brigade
Royal Engineer Detachment from 6 Commando
Observers from MI9
Press unit of war correspondents

Total Military Forces personnel: 51 officers and 525 other ranks

Air Force
Ten Hampden bombers from 50 Squadron
Blenheims and Beaufighters from 235, 236, 248, 254 and 404 Squadrons
19 Blenheims from 114 Squadron

centre for the raid. Both force commanders would be based on board, able to contact all of their commands simultaneously from a centralized operations base.

Three of the latest 'O' class destroyers were allocated to Operation *Archery* to protect its fleet of vessels whilst at sea. These would also engage enemy targets ashore and provide anti-aircraft fire to help ward off the Luftwaffe. HMS *Onslow*, *Oribi* and *Offa* each had four 4.7in guns, four 2-pdr cannon and eight 20mm anti-aircraft guns. All had entered service earlier in the year and, with a top speed of 36 knots, they were extremely fast and manoeuvrable. A fourth destroyer, HMS *Chiddingfold*, was a Type II escort destroyer launched in early March 1941. Her main firepower was expressed in six 4in guns mounted in pairs with anti-aircraft cover provided by four 2-pdr pom-pom anti-aircraft guns. In addition to their protection and bombardment duties, two of these destroyers would also move into the inshore waters of Ulvesund and attack any enemy ships, either capturing or sinking those that they found.

Two other surface vessels would take part in the operation. These were the troop-carrying ex-North Sea ferries HMS *Prince Charles* and HMS *Prince Leopold*. Both ships would carry commandos over to Norway and then disembark them into landing craft for the assault. The submarine HMS *Tuna* was also involved in the attack. It was vital that the exact position at the entrance to Vaagsfjord was reached at the appropriate time. This part of Norway was like any other part of the mountainous coastline, and the attack convoy could not rely on just dead reckoning during the night crossing of the North Sea to arrive at the exact point at the correct time. It was therefore decided that HMS *Tuna* would be stationed off Vaagsfjord in advance of the attack convoy, keeping station as a marker buoy, pinpointing the correct approaches to the target for R Adm Burrough's fleet of ships.

The warships carrying out the operation would be in great danger from enemy aircraft during the raid. They would be confined to inshore waters in daylight, with little room to manoeuvre. Their static presence would provide tempting targets to the Luftwaffe's dive-bombers and fighters. It was therefore important that an air umbrella was placed over the warships by the RAF to ward off enemy interference. Not surprisingly, there were many problems for the RAF in providing this air cover. The two nearest air bases to Vaagso – Sumburgh on the Shetland islands and Wick on the mainland of Scotland – were 250 and 400 miles away respectively. This meant that the round trip alone would be between 500 and 800 miles, not taking in account time and fuel spent circling the area under attack to repel the enemy. RAF Coastal Command did, however, have a number of Beaufighter and Blenheim fighters with sufficient range to reach Vaagso from these bases and so was able to provide four squadrons of aircraft for the task. These would work in rotation, with new fighters arriving over the area just as those patrolling there would be leaving for home.

In addition to fighter protection, the RAF also provided bombers to attack enemy airfields and to soften up the defences on the island. RAF 50 Squadron would provide ten Hampden bombers to attack enemy batteries near Vaagso and six Stirling bombers of Bomber Command to hit the German airfields at Herdla and Stavanger early on the day of the raid. Also provided were 19 Blenheim bomber variants from 110 and 114 Squadrons to attack the airfields again and strike at enemy coastal shipping, in order to draw off more of the Luftwaffe's strength.

LtCol Durnford-Slater visited COHQ in late November to learn of the fine details of the intended raid. The tasks required of his assault force were explained to him and Mountbatten asked if he believed that the attack would be successful. It was, suggested Mountbatten, an ambitious undertaking and he thought that perhaps the defended locality might be too strong for Durnford-Slater's force. The colonel was confident that with sufficient air and naval bombardment to help eliminate German strongpoints, he and his men could get ashore and be more than a match for any German garrison holding the area. Mountbatten was pleased with Durnford-Slater's reply and remained convinced that the outcome of this, the first big raid under his stewardship as head of Combined Operations, would be a successful one.

The objectives of Durnford-Slater's attack force were now refined and itemized in order to be briefed down to the individuals taking part in the operation. The main body of troops was to be carried over to Norway on board the two transport ships HMS *Prince Charles* and HMS *Prince Leopold*, with others taking passage with HMS *Oribi*. The force was divided into five groups, each with an individual set of objectives:

- Group 1 would land one troop from 3 Commando near Hollevik and clear the area of Halnoesvik and the nearby German gun site. Once these tasks had been completed, the group was to move along the coastal road to South Vaagso and form the reserve for Group 2.
- Group 2 itself contained the main body of the attacking force and consisted of three troops from 3 Commando. It would come ashore immediately south-west of the main built-up area of South Vaagso. It would then attack through the town, clearing out the enemy and demolishing industrial units, factories and buildings strategic to the Germans.
- Group 3, with the final two troops from 3 Commando, would assault and clear the island of Maaloy, attacking the main German gun battery, barracks and fish oil factories.
- Group 4 contained the two troops from 2 Commando and was the floating reserve under the personal control of Brig Haydon. This group would be introduced into the battle as and when required.
- Group 5 would land a section of commandos further up the Ulvesund to cut communications along the coastal road, entering Vaagso from the north, and it would send a fighting patrol into the small village of North Vaagso to clear it of the enemy.

The plan of attack would involve the troop transports arriving behind a headland, out of sight and range of the German gun battery on Maaloy, to disembark the commandos into landing craft just before dawn. HMS *Kenya*

16 DECEMBER 1941

Operation commanders briefed onboard HMS *Kenya*

and its accompanying destroyers would then bombard all known enemy positions. Under cover of this fire, the landing craft would approach their landing places. This would coincide with a bombing attack by Hampdens of the RAF. Smoke would then be placed over the landing sites and the bombardment continue until stopped by signal flares fired by Durnford-Slater's men just as they were about to land.

The headquarters for military operations was under the control of Brig Haydon and would remain throughout the raid onboard HMS *Kenya*. It was an arrangement that would allow the military and naval commanders to keep in close touch with each other. Post-raid reports made special mention of these arrangements: 'A cruiser makes an excellent headquarters ship for a small formation', it noted. 'The bridge is the best place from which to control military operations not only on account of the view obtained, but also it is in immediate touch with all signaling and wireless terminals. This advantage, combined with the first class signal facilities, overbalances the unfavourable conditions of wireless interference and gunfire blasts.' It might be a noisy environment when *Kenya*'s 6in guns opened fire, but it was an admirable position from which to organize a battle.

German defences around Vaagso were extensive, but not too formidable. The main enemy gun battery on Maaloy Island at the entrance to Ulvesund consisted of four German 10.5cm guns in open pits. Situated four miles to the south-east was another coastal artillery site at Rugsundo Island, with three 13.5cm Russian guns. This battery could also bring fire on warships approaching Maaloy. Both of these batteries had to be neutralized by direct naval fire and bombing raids made just prior to the landings. The raid on Rugsundo was scheduled to start as the warships began their western approach up Vaagsfjord, for they had to pass the German lookout station at Husevaag, and it was thought that the bombing to the east would divert attention away from the passing naval vessels. A further coast battery at the northern end of Ulvesund at Halsoer was not thought to be a danger, for the intervening mountains in the centre of Vaagso Island would prevent fire from there reaching the site of the landings.

The second week in December saw the assembling of forces for Operation *Archery*. The naval force, with the exception of the destroyers *Onslow* and *Chiddingfold* which would arrive later, gathered at Scapa Flow along with more and more of the ground forces. By 15 December, Durnford-Slater's force was complete and had arrived from their assembly point on the Clyde in the troop transports *Prince Charles* and *Prince Leopold*. On 16 December all commanders met onboard HMS *Kenya* for a briefing. Rumours were rife that an operation was about to take place, and it was thought important that everyone be kept occupied. Two rehearsals were planned to involve all arms and all three services. The first of these, Exercise 'L', was carried out at dawn on 17 December. Amphibious landings were made on a small island in Scapa Flow that was similar in size to Maaloy. Under the cover of a naval bombardment and through smoke laid by Hampden bombers, Durnford-Slater's commando force landed on the Holm of Howton. Much valuable experience was gained, as the commandos made their attack under

PRIVATE, NO. 4 TROOP, 3 COMMANDO

1. Life jacket
2. Toggle rope
3. Thompson sub-machine gun
4. Lee Enfield Rifle No. 4

Commandos priming grenades onboard their transport ship. The arming of weapons took place in the last few hours before the assault in order to minimize the chances of accidents. (IWM, N503)

conditions similar to those that would be found in battle. The exercise went smoothly and morale became sky high.

The elimination of the enemy battery on Maaloy was the key objective of the opening phase of the raid, so the opportunity was taken by Admiral Burrough's flagship and the RAF to further rehearse its destruction. HMS *Kenya*, in conjunction with Hampden bombers, carried out a practice bombardment on a dummy battery at Stack Skerry to coordinate timings and objectives for the final mission. A further combined rehearsal involving all forces, Exercise 'L2', was later postponed due to bad weather. The practice landings could not go ahead, but *Kenya* and the RAF once again cooperated in their final rehearsal during another dummy attack on Stack Skerry. Everything so far had gone according to plan and expectations were high that all events and timetables would mesh together completely on the day to ensure an effective amphibious landing.

With the seaborne and amphibious parts of the raid having been effectively rehearsed by the commandos, it was time to get familiar with the specific targets allocated to each troop. A complete scale model of Vaagso had been made by Combined Operations' planners based on reconnaissance photographs and intelligence reports, so the commandos could study the layout of streets in the town. Every house, factory and building was shown, although the names of the targets were withheld for security reasons. Over the next few days, each group studied the area in great detail, familiarizing itself with every twist and turn of the road, every likely building that could hold the enemy and every target earmarked for demolition. The groups rehearsed their approaches and withdrawals, each commander itemized every step they would take, every NCO considered what was to be done if his officer should fall, and each man was instructed on where and when he should act. Every detail of the attack was carefully worked out.

Whilst they were ashore on Vaagso, the commandos would need enough weapons, equipment and ammunition to last the whole of their time in action. Each of the commandos would carry 100 rounds of ammunition and every Bren gun crew would have 50 magazines available. Virtually everyone would help carry the Bren gun magazines ashore, so they could be stockpiled for use as and when required. The same was true for mortar bombs to feed the 3in mortars. Officers would all carry 25 rounds of pistol ammunition for their personal side arms, although Durnford-Slater felt himself vulnerable with only a puny pistol as defence. Demolition parties were formed from the engineers present with each group. These sappers were trained to sabotage the factories and installations used by the enemy.

As we have seen, the destruction of the fish oil factories was just one of the objectives of the raid. The attack was also planned to destroy the enemy in Vaagso and the surrounding areas, especially those on the island of Maaloy. Aerial reconnaissance and intelligence gathered from the Norwegian underground had identified most of the buildings used by the Germans. These would be attacked and demolished where possible, as would much of the town's infrastructure. Earmarked for destruction were the telephone exchange, the wireless telegraphy station alongside the harbour, the German headquarters lodged in the Ulvesund Hotel, the billets used by German soldiers, the barracks on Maaloy and all German offices in Vaagso.

It was also important that all Norwegian collaborators were arrested and brought back to Britain. These quislings were hated by the Free Norwegians based in London, and it was important that those helping the German war effort in Norway were seen to be punished by their fellow countrymen. The spiriting away of collaborators would also have an effect on others in the country who were tempted to help the Germans. If it could be seen that the British could land in Norway and arrest quislings at will, they might be more reluctant to volunteer their services.

Although the original date given for the landings at Vaagso and the Lofoten Islands was 21 December, various delays caused this date to be put back to dawn on 26 December. The ships of Operation *Archery* would put into Sullom Voe on the Shetland Islands for refuelling. Those of Operation *Anklet*, Force J, had their own oil tankers and would proceed directly to their target. Sailing dates were 24 December for *Archery* and 22 December for *Anklet*, as the latter's forces had further to sail.

THE RAID

On 22 December 1941, Force 'J' left Scapa Flow for the Lofoten Islands. Operation *Anklet*'s fleet of 20 vessels – the destroyer HMS *Wheatland* and the transport HMS *Princess Josephine Charlotte* were to join the convoy from the Shetlands – set sail to the north through a gathering sea and ploughed their way towards their target. Three days later, on Christmas Day, the flagship HMS *Arethusa* made signal contact with the submarine *Tigris*. The submarine was waiting to mark the route into the channel that led into the seaways off the Lofoten Islands. The next day, just before dawn, the fleet entered Vestfjord at 0751hrs and began to disperse. Several hundred miles south of them, the ships of Operation *Archery* were also at sea, but they had not had such a calm and orderly passage towards their destination of Vaagso.

The Approach

Three days after Force 'J' had left, R Adm Burrough brought his line of ships out from Scapa Flow into a steadily worsening North Sea at 2115hrs. The passage to the Sullom Voe anchorage in the Shetland Islands was a rough one. The two ex-North Sea ferries fared particularly badly and began taking on water as gale force winds whipped up the seas. A signal was made to all vessels to reduce speed and the ships tried to hold course as best they could. The next morning, when they arrived at the Shetlands, the two troopships were in a bad shape. Both of them had been damaged. The *Prince Charles* was found to have taken on more than 140 tons of water and its forward compartments flooded to a depth of 14ft. The *Prince Leopold* suffered similar damage, including buckled bulkheads and dented superstructure. Not surprisingly, most of the commandos below decks were violently seasick.

It was clear that emergency repairs would have to be made to the two troopships. These would inevitably take some time, even though the main object was just to patch up the worst damage and make the vessels seaworthy. The weather forecast was also unpromising, with more winter gales sweeping in that day from the west. R Adm Burrough reluctantly gave

Men of 3 Commando in their assault landing craft still slung from davits onboard the transport ship HMS *Prince Leopold*, waiting for R Adm Burrough to give the order to begin the attack. (IWM, N499)

the order for the attack to be postponed for 24 hours. Christmas Day would be spent not at sea as expected, but in the sheltered waters of Sullom Voe.

At 1400hrs on the 26th, just as Force 'J' was making its presence felt in the Lofotens, the ships of Operation *Archery* once again set sail for Norway. Fortunately, the weather had moderated to allow the ships to continue their passage as scheduled and to arrive off the coast the next day in perfect conditions. Contact was made with the submarine *Tuna* in the early morning darkness, allowing Burrough to line up his convoy right on position four miles from the entrance of Vaagsfjord close by Klovning Island. It was 0739hrs, one minute later that planned.

The speed of the vessels now dropped considerably. On the bridge of the *Kenya*, the Norwegian pilot guided Burrough's ships steadily and almost silently towards the entrance of Vaagsfjord. Minutes passed slowly as the warships closed inexorably on their goal, passing into the mouth of the fjord. Then the low hum of approaching aircraft signalled the arrival of friendly forces.

Hampden bombers from RAF 50 Squadron swept over the flotilla of ships and flew up the fjord, heading for the coastal artillery site on Rugsundo five miles beyond the opening to Ulvesund. They passed over the island of Husevaag with its German naval look-out post on the southern edge of Vaagsfjord and continued with their bombing run. It was hoped that the

24 DECEMBER 1941

Operation *Archery* forces set out

One of the most famous images from Operation *Archery* – a still photograph taken from film of the raid, hence its grainy nature. The image shows commandos ashore on Maaloy Island just after landing, moving through the smoke screen laid by Hampden bombers. (IWM, N520)

presence of these bombers flying low over the observation post would divert enemy attention skywards away from the warships sliding quietly up the fjord. No signal lamp pierced the gloom and no shot rang out, which led Burrough to believe that the lookouts had not spotted his flotilla. *Kenya* and the other ships now slipped quietly into the inland waters of the fjord. On either side of the vessels, great snow-covered mountains began looming high above them, giving those on deck the sense of entering a long white tunnel.

The noise of the bombing raid on Rugsundo echoed across the water, diverting all attention to the east. Long waving lines of anti-aircraft tracer snaked across the sky as the guns on surrounding hills opened up on the bombers. Burrough's ships had in fact been spotted by the lookout post on Husevaag, and details were immediately telegraphed across to the German harbour master at South Vaagso. No alarm was raised, however, for a small coastal convoy had been expected and it was assumed that the ships entering the fjord were friendly.

Once inside the fjord, the warships began to take up their stations prior to opening the bombardment, with the destroyer HMS *Chiddingfold* escorting the two troopships away to port towards the tiny bay south of Hollevik. The bay afforded some shelter, as it was set behind a great headland out of sight of the enemy battery on Maaloy. Here the ships' crews could load and lower the assault boats that would take the commandos to their objectives in relative safety. Meanwhile, HMS *Kenya* led the bombardment force round to the north-east to line up with the entrance to the Ulvesund for a clear sight on the enemy gun positions on Maaloy. HMS *Onslow* closed on *Kenya*'s starboard quarter and *Offa* came up astern of the flagship. HMS *Oribi* remained near the entrance to the fjord, to cover the force from the west.

By 0835hrs, the crews of the *Prince Charles* and *Prince Leopold* had completed the loading of the commandos into their assault landing craft, ready for their run ashore. A signal was sent to the force commander on

Troops move through South Vaagso at the start of the raid, with evidence of the smoke screen still in evidence. (IWM, N515)

board *Kenya* that all was ready. Burrough replied with the order to cast off and at 0842hrs the boats were released. They formed up in two lines, with those from *Prince Charles* who were to attack South Vaagso to the north and those from *Prince Leopold* destined to land on Maaloy to the south. It was now time for the warships to fire the opening salvoes in the attack on Vaagso.

Bombardment and Landings

HMS *Kenya* moved slowly through the dim light of dawn towards Maaloy and its defences. At 0848hrs, the cruiser fired a number of star shells over the island, illuminating the scene with brilliant white light. Almost immediately, it then opened fire with its two forward 6in turrets as the cruiser slowly continued around the headland into the Ulvesund. With the island now fully in sight, the captain of the *Kenya* brought his vessel sideways-on to its objective, opening fire with all four turrets both fore and aft. A great broadside erupted in clouds of smoke and flame as 12 shells screamed across the still waters and smashed into the gun battery and the flimsy wooden buildings that surrounded it. *Onslow* then moved slowly ahead to come abreast of the cruiser to join in the bombardment with its own broadsides. Then it was the turn of *Offa* as it too slipped into position on the port side of HMS *Kenya*,

Behind and to port, two long lines of landing craft edged their way forward on their run-in to shore. Once round the headland, two of the left-hand craft containing Lt Clements and his Group 1 peeled off and headed for a landing place close to Hollevik. They touched ground on a very rocky stretch of the shoreline and were quickly ashore and about their business, looking for the suspected gun emplacement on the high ground near Halnoesvik. The other craft continued closing on their objectives.

Things were now happening very quickly. The battery at Rugsundo suddenly came to life in spite of the aerial bombardment that had been

27 DECEMBER 1941

0739hrs Operation *Archery* forces arrive at Vaagso

showered down on it by the Hampden bombers. One gun had been knocked out but another, better protected by significant earthworks, survived the attack, and as the Hampdens turned away its crew left their shelters and returned to their weapon. Eight minutes after *Kenya* had begun its bombardment, the battery at Rugsundo opened fire on the British cruiser. The gunnery was slow and erratic, but a nuisance none the less. The cruiser swung one of her turrets away from Maaloy and returned fire with salvoes of 6in shells. The German gunners managed a few more rounds and then fell silent. In the meantime, Maaloy was slowly being shattered by a great weight of high explosive from the warships. None of its guns came into action, for surprise had been complete. The German gun crews were still in barracks when *Kenya*'s first shells struck home. From then on, the pounding was continuous. Twenty naval guns from three ships dropped over 400 shells onto an area of less than 300 square yards in just nine minutes.

As these shells slammed into the German defences, the assault craft carrying LtCol Durnford-Slater and Group 2 chugged their way towards their landing beach at South Vaagso. The gap between the impact of the shells and the boats began closing fast and it soon became time for a halt to be called to the bombardment. In the lead boat, the colonel reached down for his Very pistol and began firing flares into the air. One after another they rose in a low curve and exploded into brilliant red light in the sky above the target. The ten flares signalled a request to cease the bombardment and were also the sign for the last of the Hampdens to begin their final task before they returned to base. Seven of the bombers dropped down in the sky and turned northwards for a low bombing run. As they came over Maaloy and

The raiders advance cautiously through South Vaagso, well aware that enemy snipers are in the buildings all around and in the hills above the town, picking off unsuspecting commandos who happen to show themselves. (IWM, N530)

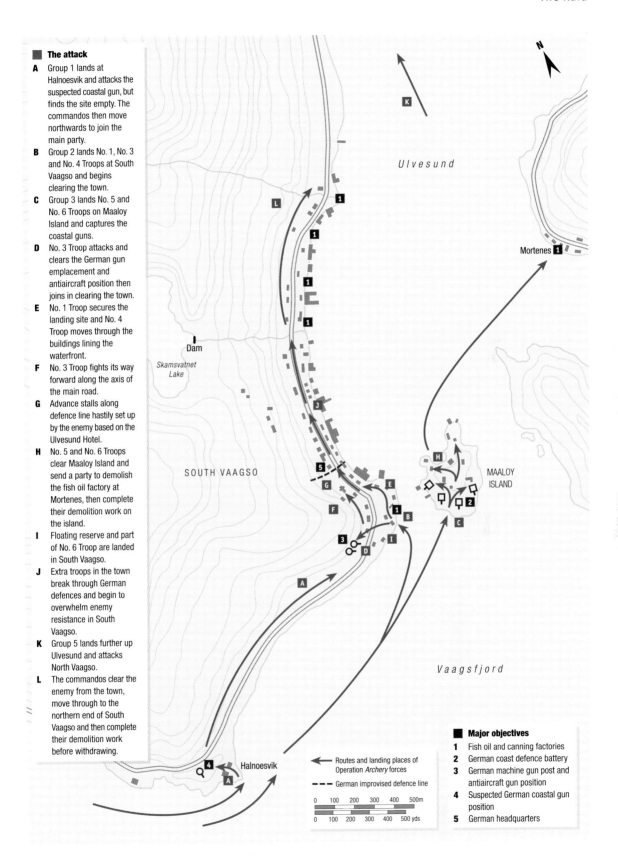

The attack

A Group 1 lands at Halnoesvik and attacks the suspected coastal gun, but finds the site empty. The commandos then move northwards to join the main party.

B Group 2 lands No. 1, No. 3 and No. 4 Troops at South Vaagso and begins clearing the town.

C Group 3 lands No. 5 and No. 6 Troops on Maaloy Island and captures the coastal guns.

D No. 3 Troop attacks and clears the German gun emplacement and antiaircraft position then joins in clearing the town.

E No. 1 Troop secures the landing site and No. 4 Troop moves through the buildings lining the waterfront.

F No. 3 Troop fights its way forward along the axis of the main road.

G Advance stalls along defence line hastily set up by the enemy based on the Ulvesund Hotel.

H No. 5 and No. 6 Troops clear Maaloy Island and send a party to demolish the fish oil factory at Mortenes, then complete their demolition work on the island.

I Floating reserve and part of No. 6 Troop are landed in South Vaagso.

J Extra troops in the town break through German defences and begin to overwhelm enemy resistance in South Vaagso.

K Group 5 lands further up Ulvesund and attacks North Vaagso.

L The commandos clear the enemy from the town, move through to the northern end of South Vaagso and then complete their demolition work before withdrawing.

Ulvesund

Mortenes

Skamsvatnet Lake

Dam

SOUTH VAAGSO

MAALOY ISLAND

Vaagsfjord

Halnoesvik

← Routes and landing places of Operation *Archery* forces

--- German improvised defence line

| 0 | 100 | 200 | 300 | 400 | 500m |
| 0 | 100 | 200 | 300 | 400 | 500 yds |

Major objectives
1 Fish oil and canning factories
2 German coast defence battery
3 German machine gun post and antiaircraft gun position
4 Suspected German coastal gun position
5 German headquarters

37

Vaagso they released bombs containing, not high explosive, but chemicals. The stability of the bombs during their descent was aided by small parachutes, but they still hit the ground hard and bounced along, burning and fizzing, releasing fragments of phosphorus in all directions. As the air came into contact with the volatile chemical, the bombs generated great clouds of thick white smoke. On Maaloy, the bombs were dropped on a front of about 270yds and, as there was virtually no wind, they soon produced a dense fog. The waterfront was quickly covered in a penetrating mist, with visibility reduced to 20yds, hiding the approaching assault craft from the eyes of those enemy soldiers who were brave enough to venture out of their barracks.

The smoke bombs dropped on South Vaagso were not so carefully placed. One aircraft in particular, hit by anti-aircraft fire, released its bombs just 55yds ahead of the landing craft. The aircraft then gradually lost height, tried to make a turn towards the warships, and crashed into the fjord. Lookouts on board *Prince Leopold* spotted the stricken bomber and the ship slipped anchor and raced to the crash site. Three of the aircraft's crew were spotted in the water and brought onboard ship. One crew member was not accounted for. Unfortunately, two of those rescued failed to respond to efforts to revive them and died. The other, its pilot F/Sgt Smith, survived.

One of the bombs from F/Sgt Smith's Hampden fell right into an assault boat containing some of No. 4 Troop, killing two men outright and spraying burning phosphorus over many others. Everyone onboard was injured, some burnt so horribly that they eventually died. Lt Komrower was lucky enough to see the bomb drifting down and was able to hurl himself into the sea to

Casualties taken on Maaloy Island were difficult to remove to safety. The rocky nature of the tiny island meant that they had to be manhandled by groups of stretcher bearers over rough ground back to the assault craft. (IWM, 457)

escape. Fires started and spread to the ammunition. Soon the craft was engulfed in flame as ammunition exploded and flares were sent flying in all directions. It was fortunate that the craft soon touched bottom. Unfortunately, when it bounced onto the beach it crushed the legs of Lt Komrower, who was holding onto the side of the boat. Men scrambled ashore, eager to escape the raging inferno. Those that were able dragged themselves and their injured comrades away from the craft. Some of the phosphorus had also sprayed over adjacent craft, starting fires on board those boats too, and peppering the occupants and their uniforms with the smouldering chemical.

In the lead boat, LtCol Durnford-Slater escaped most this confusion as his assault craft landed amongst the boulders on the stony foreshore 220yds south-west of the outskirts of the town. His group were hidden from the enemy beneath a rocky cliff face around 33ft high. One of the smoke bombs that had landed on the ground at the top of the cliff showered him with burning phosphorus. His tunic caught fire, but he was able to beat out the flames with his gloved hands. Behind him the other landing craft slid into shore. Slater ordered the burning boat to be pushed away from the narrow beach and organized help for the wounded. Some were dealt with by 3 Commando's medical officer, Capt Corry; others were loaded onto the assault boats and returned to the mother ships.

A commando watches as the German barracks on Maaloy and its associated ammunition dump are set ablaze. (IWM, N466)

27 DECEMBER 1941

0848hrs Bombardment of Maaloy commences

So far the landings had been virtually unopposed. Some enemy fire from a machine gun in the town had been aimed at the landing craft during the final few yards of the run in, but most of this had passed over the commandos as they closed on the rocky foreshore. The men of Group 2 now made their move up the cliff towards the town, and set about the task of eliminating the enemy. The thick smog helped them to get onto the road that runs through the town. Inland from this feature, the ground rose sharply into almost vertical cliffs of rock that led back to the high mountains in the interior of the island.

Just to the north of Group 2's landing place was a German strongpoint that helped guard the entrance to Ulvesund. Nearby was an anti-aircraft position. These became the initial objectives of Capt Giles and his No. 3 Troop whilst Capt Bradley and his No. 1 Troop secured the landing place. Giles' men attacked the strongpoint with great vigour, rushing into their first action of the war just as they had rehearsed in exercises over and over again. Every bound forward was covered by fire, allowing the commandos to close on the German position with speed. Very soon the strongpoint's leader, Oberleutnant Bremer, was killed along with many other defenders. Command was passed to Stabsfeldwebel Lebrenz, but he too soon fell. With the loss of their leaders, German resistance at the strongpoint ended and the position was taken. Giles' troop secured the area and then moved down onto the main road and entered the town.

LtCol Durnford-Slater set up his headquarters near the landing place. With him was his signals officer, Lt Head, the adjutant, Capt Smallman and the administration officer, Capt Martin. Communications proved to be problematic, for the No. 18 radio sets with each troop worked only intermittently. The link back to Brig Haydon's command post on *Kenya* also worked only spasmodically. These were problems that continued to plague many other Allied raids during World War II, and were never really resolved until more reliable equipment was developed later in the war. Contact with the forward troops was mainly carried out by runners, who took messages to and fro throughout the day.

South Vaagso

South Vaagso consisted of just one main street around half a mile long, on either side of which were scattered wooden houses and a few public buildings. The road ran parallel to the fjord about 50yds inland from the water's edge. All the fish oil factories fronted onto the fjord, with wooden jetties jutting out into the water from which the fish was landed. Each of these factories had been identified for demolition. The men of Group 2 from No. 3 and No. 4 Troops each now set about their tasks, slipping into the town through the gradually dispersing cover of the smoke to do battle with the German garrison. They moved methodically from building to building, seeking out the enemy whilst all the while trying to reassure Norwegian civilians they would be safe if they remained under cover. Capt Giles' No. 3 Troop used the road as its axis of advance, whilst Capt Forrester and his depleted No. 4 Troop moved through the buildings and alleyways to the right along the waterfront.

With the attack well underway, the assault craft were given over to ferrying in ammunition and bringing out wounded men. Here mortar bombs are being loaded onto one of the small craft from the mother ship. (IWM, N501)

It was not long before the Germans holed up in the town came to life and began countering these moves. Some of the enemy were still in the buildings in which they were quartered, and began sniping the commandos as they approached. The battle for South Vaagso developed into a protracted and difficult one, for each building had to be stalked from cover and entered with bravery whilst sniper fire came at the commandos from all directions. Some German riflemen had sought cover in the rocky features above the town, and now took leisurely pot shots at any British soldier they spotted moving between the buildings. The source of this fire was difficult to locate for the men creeping along the main street. All seemed quiet until suddenly a man would fall dead from a shot fired by an unseen assassin up in the hills. Every corner that was rounded brought the commandos into a possible new line of fire. It took great ingenuity and determination for the advance through the town to continue.

Misfortune befell Operation *Archery* just before the raid, when new German troops arrived in the town. Around fifty of the enemy had been allowed leave in South Vaagso over Christmas and came into the town for some rest and recreation from their normal lonely outposts elsewhere. These soldiers were veterans of the action that took place during the invasion of Norway in 1940. They were all well versed in the art of street fighting and now bolstered the German garrison at an inopportune moment for the British. The enemy fought tenaciously for each structure, often remaining hidden inside whilst British troops were in the process of clearing the building room by room.

27 DECEMBER 1941

0857hrs Commandos begin landing

Attack on Maaloy

Landing simultaneously with Group 2 were the troops of Maj Jack Churchill's Group 3. Maj Churchill was 3 Commando's second-in-command, and he was given one of the most important first tasks of the raid, the silencing of the four coastal guns on Maaloy. The warships could bombard the gun emplacements as long as they liked, but it would still take troops on the ground to render them useless, along with their detachments of enemy troops. Churchill had with him two troops of commandos with which to accomplish the task: Capt Ronald's No. 5 Troop and Capt Peter Young's No. 6 Troop. Each troop was given specific objectives once they had landed. Capt Ronald's commandos were to seize the gun on the extreme right and then sweep up the eastern side of the island to capture and destroy the enemy ammunition dump and demolish the fish oil factory on the northern shore. Capt Young's task was to capture and destroy the three enemy guns on the left of the landings and then clear the remainder of the island, including the German barracks.

Jack Churchill was one of the commandos' most flamboyant characters. He had a reputation for eccentric behaviour that earned him the nickname 'Mad Jack'. He often went into battle dressed in a kilt and carrying a broadsword. In the campaign in France in 1940, he even had with him a longbow. It was alleged that he had actually killed a German with his bow during the retreat to Dunkirk, probably the first time an enemy of England had been killed with such a weapon since medieval times. His exploits won him the Military Cross, but his larger than life activities and reckless courage often made his behaviour rather unpredictable.

As Group 3 approached their landing places on Maaloy, now covered in smoke by the RAF bombers, Churchill again put on a spectacular performance. Standing in the blunt prow of the landing craft carrying No. 6

Street fighting in South Vaagso progressed slowly through the town, each building having to be completely cleared of the enemy before moving on to the next. (IWM, N488)

Troop, he led his men into battle with some music played on his bagpipes. The Scotsmen amongst the boats were stirred by this martial music, although some of the Sassenach members of his group couldn't wait to get clear of what they felt was a hideous wailing.

The right-hand sector of the landing beach was covered by a German machine gun, and as soon as No. 5 Troop touched down on the rocky foreshore a section of commandos dashed off in this direction to silence the gun. Running on instinct, they burst through the smoke screen along the water's edge and emerged almost on top of the weapon pit. A burst of Tommy-gun fire eliminated the three startled Germans manning the weapon and the post remained silent. The gun's three-man crew had not even managed to get a single shot off before they were destroyed.

The remainder of Capt Ronald's troop moved off from their assault craft looking for the right-hand coastal gun. The mist created by the smoke bombs made progress difficult and constant direction hard to keep. They pressed on and soon ran into the barbed wire that surrounded the gun site. They had expected some German reaction to the assault and were apprehensive that none had appeared. The wire entanglement was easy to deal with and Capt Reynolds and his men brushed their way through it to discover the gun pit and its associated artillery piece. They now took command of the weapon and looked for the enemy who should be manning it. None were to be seen.

Capt Peter Young and his No. 6 Troop had a similar experience. His troop was split into two sections. The left-hand section, commanded by Lt Wills, made its way over the rocks and up the slight cliff lining the water's edge and disappeared into the smoke, probing their way forward looking for the two guns on the extreme left. Like those commandos in No. 5 Troop, Wills and his men found the barbed wire defences and the pits containing the guns to be unmanned. Both guns were taken without a shot being fired, and a guard was placed over them. The troop commander experienced the same situation when capturing the gun in the centre. Peter Young and his men were expecting that at least a machine gun would be covering the wire defences around the gun, but there was nothing. Where was the enemy?

In the meantime, Jack Churchill had streaked off the landing craft, up the cliff and into the smoke, brandishing a sword and hollering loudly. Since then he had not been seen by anyone in Group 3, including his batman, Guardsman Stretton. The smoke was still thick along the water's edge and contact had been lost between all three parties as soon as they had entered the mist. When Capt Young, however, fired a white Very light into the air to signify that his gun had been captured, he was encouraged to see two other lights in the sky – one to his west and one to his east – showing that those guns too had been captured.

Young stopped for moment to give his men a short rest, sheltering behind the low stone wall of the pit. The smoke was by then beginning to thin and a few buildings could be seen ahead in the gloom. After a short while, the enemy made their presence felt and a grenade was heard to explode away to the right. Then, from some huts around 200yds ahead, some Germans started to make a move. The first of the enemy running towards the

OVERLEAF: Unlike previous commando raids, the Vaagso operation involved heavy fighting in a built-up area immediately after landing. The enemy held South Vaagso in force and the commandos knew that they would have to confront their foe at very close quarters with just the light weapons they carried. They moved through the streets and buildings in the face of accurate small arms and sniper fire, winkling out the enemy from the factories and houses that lined the route of their advance. The fighting became extremely localized with whole sections often working in unison to eliminate an individual German who barred their way. At Vaagso the war became personal, with the troops on both sides stalking each other looking for the opportunity to kill.

commandos was felled with a single bullet from Young. Two others slipped into a hut away to the right and were flushed out by a few grenades thrown through the window. They surrendered without returning fire. Then once again everything fell quiet.

Just eight minutes had passed since the landings, and the German garrison on the island and those supposed to be manning the guns were still in their shelters. Hauptmann Butziger and some of his men were still unsure that the bombing and shelling were over, and remained inside one of the buildings, unaware that the commandos had landed. Capt Young's men discovered them as they advanced inland from the gun battery. The Germans were suddenly confronted with a determined group of enemy, and tamely filed into captivity without a shot being fired. Both troops of commandos from Group 3 found the same lack of resistance across the island. Whilst a few of the enemy put up some sort of resistance and died fighting, most individuals and even whole groups were winkled out of their hiding places without opposition, and virtually all of them were suffering from shock. The Germans had been totally demoralized by the ferocity of the naval bombardment and willingly gave up the fight. Towards the northern end of Maaloy, a little more resistance was met. Capt Young had a brief close-quarters encounter with two Germans as he rounded a corner. They were near enough to be bayoneted, but the quick-thinking Tpr Clark despatched them both with his Tommy gun.

Young eventually came across the battery commander's office, and was anxious to capture any German documents that were inside. Unfortunately the building was on fire. Young and a few of his men therefore formed a human chain inside, grabbing any papers they could find and throwing them out the window. They had no idea what was important, and so continued stripping the building as fast as the flames would let them. A halt was called to the proceedings when the captain's tunic began smouldering.

Maj 'Mad' Jack Churchill, 3 Commando's second-in-command, inspects a German gun on Maaloy after its capture by the men of Capt Young's No. 6 Troop. (IWM, N463)

46

Meanwhile, as the troops fanned out across the island, ensuring a complete end to the opposition, the demolition teams began their work on the German emplacements, petrol tanks, ammunition store, barracks and other buildings and the two fish oil factories. Soon the whole island was aflame. By then Maj Churchill had rejoined his men from his solo exploits and organized a headquarters group, receiving situation reports as runners came in from all over the island, each reporting their successes. At 0920hrs, Churchill signalled the command post on HMS *Kenya* and reported to Brig Haydon that the battery and the entire island had been secured.

Assault through the Town

Once Capt Bradley's troop had the area around Group 2's landings at South Vaagso secured, he took some of his men into the town to deal with his next objective. No. 1 Troop had the task of organizing the demolition of targeted buildings once Nos 3 and 4 Troops had captured them. Bradley and his men now moved to the first of their assignments, the large fish oil factory close by the landing place. It was in this building that the first of the quislings was arrested – he was the factory owner and had collaborated freely with the enemy. He was not the last of the quislings to be arrested and taken back to the ships that day.

The first of the groups to achieve their objectives was Group 1 under Lt Clements. He and his men had been the first of the commandos to land near Hollevik on the extreme left of the assault. Their landing place was overlooked by a large white house from which a few shots were fired. The house was stormed and two Germans wounded as they fled out the rear. There was no other opposition to the group and the men quickly set about clearing the area. The suspected gun emplacement was found to be empty. At 0950hrs, with the area secured, Clements tried to contact Durnford-Slater for further instructions. He was unable to raise his CO, but was able to talk

Signallers trying to make contact with Force Headquarters on HMS *Kenya*. Radio traffic was often disrupted through the unreliability of the equipment carried on the raid. It was not until much later in the war that more effective and reliable signalling equipment was produced. (IWM, N541)

27 DECEMBER 1941

0920hrs 'Island secured' signal set from Maaloy

to Brig Haydon back at the command post on HMS *Kenya*. The brigadier ordered Clements to take his No. 2 Troop along the main road into South Vaagso and act as reserve for the main body of Group 2.

Moving through the buildings along the waterfront in South Vaagso with No. 4 Troop was Capt Martin Linge of the 1st Norwegian Independent Company, accompanied by Sgt Ruben Larsen and a Private Veeda. They had two main objectives, to liaise with the British and Norwegian civilians and to capture those quislings who had been identified locally or who were on the SOE list of collaborators. Capt Linge also wished to kill as many Germans as possible and to capture any documents that might be of use to the British.

Linge and his men had a free hand to complete their tasks, as Sgt Larsen explained in his report made after the raid: 'Our plan was that we were to work independently of the British troops. We took a lot of chances in dashing across roads and fields, which the others would not risk. We risked it with Capt Linge and were very lucky, however, Capt Linge's intention was to advance so quickly that we reached the German Headquarters before they had time to dispose of documents and papers.'

The German headquarters that Linge and his men were hoping to capture was in the Ulvesund Hotel, which was situated midway along the main street. It was a prominent building and one which he knew was bound to contain a number of Germans. Unfortunately, the closer that Capt Forrester's No. 4 Troop got to the hotel, the stiffer the German resistance became. The German naval harbourmaster, Leutnant zur See Sebelin had taken over responsibility for the defence of the town and had organized all the servicemen around his headquarters into a scratch force. He arranged these men into an improvised defensive line based around the hotel to bar any further movement northwards by the commandos.

A 3in mortar team goes into action in the streets of South Vaagso, attempting to lob bombs down on a troublesome enemy position whilst staying out of sight of snipers. (IWM, N5330

Forrester's troop was therefore having a difficult time on the right of the advance. The captain had lost two of his officers during the attack – Lt Komrower on the assault craft and Lt Lloyd shot in the neck by a sniper. Forrester moved forward at the head of his men, throwing grenades into buildings and firing a Tommy gun from the hip. Racing from house to house, the commandos burst through doors and charged inside, clearing the buildings room by room. Sometimes they were confronted by terrified civilians, sometimes challenged by a burst from a light weapon fired by a retreating German or by a stick grenade lobbed through a window from outside. Some commandos went in by the front door, whilst others slipped over fences at the back to cut off any escape routes, catching fleeing Germans with rifle fire. It was a slow, hard and dangerous progress through the town.

The advance was just as tough for the troop moving up the left side of the main street. Capt Giles' No. 3 Troop was met by enemy resistance in a large house soon after it began its advance. The enemy infantry inside defied all attempts to evict them from the building. A welter of fire from rifles, Brens and Tommy guns ripped through the windows and doors of the building. Eventually, frustrated by a lack of progress, Capt Giles led a mad dash for the front entrance of the house. He burst through the doorway with his men tumbling in behind him. Mad with rage, the commandos went from room to room, tossing in grenades and spraying the rooms with small-arms fire. Those of the enemy who were still able, fled out through the back door, chased away by long bursts of fire. Giles followed after them, only to fall immediately from a bullet in the stomach. A wounded German lying outside had managed to get one shot off before he too was eliminated by the commandos who were following their captain.

Fire then hit the troop from the snipers lodged in the hills. Lt Hall was hit and fell to the ground. Two men who went to his aid were also cut down,

Signallers on Maaloy Island communicate with 3 Commando's headquarters prior to sending reinforcements over to help with the street fighting. (IWM, N482)

49

killed by the same snipers who had shot the lieutenant. Command passed to Capt Giles' younger brother Bruce, but he was momentarily in a state of shock at seeing his brother killed and the attack gradually lost its momentum.

Over to the right, Capt Forrester brought his No. 4 Troop up to the area of the Ulvesund Hotel. At this time, Forrester did not know that the hotel had become the mainstay of the improvised defence line organized by Leutnant Sebelin. The captain thought that the best method of attack would be a sudden rush at the front of the building with all guns blazing, relying on momentum to carry them into the hotel once the doors were blown.

Forrester led the assault. He dashed across the street, urging his men forward. He almost reached the front door and was ready to lob a grenade towards it when he was shot by one of the enemy inside. He fell forward onto the grenade that he had primed in his hand. A few seconds later the bomb went off underneath his slumped body. The death of their commander sent a ripple of shock through the attackers. Fire from inside the building hit a couple of other men, and the assault force retired back across the street.

Arriving near the hotel was Capt Linge with his sergeant and corporal. A few others of his company who were acting as liaison with No. 4 Troop had also joined them. With the death of Capt Forrester the troop was now without any officers. Linge immediately took charge of No. 4 Troop. Sgt Larsen later described a fresh assault on the German headquarters:

> On the way, we met some troops who had lost their leader and Capt Linge said he would take charge of them. We decided to try and take the Ulvesund Hotel and Capt Linge ordered us to throw hand grenades into the building. After this had been done, we were to rush into the house and take what we wanted, while other troops were to return to our base with the message that the hotel had been taken. Capt Linge was very keen on doing this, but he did not take into consideration the fact that the troops did not like the idea at all. When we reached the hotel we discovered that there were still a lot of Germans there. We retreated and went round a corner where we stopped for a few seconds.

Linge decided to make another assault on the hotel hoping that the momentum of the attack would carry them through. He regrouped his men beside a building close by and then ordered a charge forward. As he rounded the corner into full view of the hotel he was immediately hit in the chest by a bullet. He stumbled forward and almost made it to the entrance. Sgt Larsen was close behind: 'Suddenly, without any warning a bullet hit Capt Linge. I tried to get him away when another was fired, probably meant for me, which also hit him. I then took cover behind the entrance to the hotel.' Linge was dead, the attack had failed and the men withdrew once again.

It now fell to Cpl White to regroup the troop and decide what to do next. The men were apprehensive about attacking what was obviously now a heavily defended post, but the loss of their leaders had stirred them up for revenge. Leutnant Sebelin and his men inside the hotel opposite were putting up a brave defence, and were determined to hold the line across the town, but fortune now shifted in favour of the attackers. Sgt Ramsay had arrived

The demolitions on Maaloy continue, with every building being set alight by explosives and incendiaries. (IWM, N486)

close by with No. 1 Troop's mortar detachment. White put out a call for help and the mortar was brought forward to aid a fresh assault.

The mortar was quickly set up and began lobbing small bombs onto the hotel. The thud of explosions and the bursts of flame in the upper rooms blew out windows and started fires inside the headquarters building. Corporal White now renewed the assault and led his men across the street and into the hotel with all guns firing. Men threw showers of grenades through windows and doors as they ran. The enemy inside expected another assault and were ready to react. After delivering a short burst of fire, they made their way out the back of the hotel to regroup in the next building, there to continue the fight.

News of the delays and stiff opposition encountered in the town had by then reached LtCol Durnford-Slater at his command post. He went forward to see the situation for himself and realized that the advance had stalled and needed new impetus. The enemy had to be cleared completely from the buildings and factories in order for the demolition work to begin, so his men had to press on, even though casualties were mounting. The attack was also starting to fall well behind schedule. Durnford-Slater knew he would have to call for more reinforcements and asked Brig Haydon to commit the floating reserve into the town. He also signalled Maj Churchill on Maaloy, asking if he could send help.

Over on Maaloy, Churchill was by then satisfied that his men were in total control of the island. The battery had been captured and its guns destroyed. The barrack area had been cleared and his men were now carrying out demolitions on the two fish oil factories, the German ammunition dump and the other buildings used by the enemy. He could now spare half of Capt Young's No. 6 Troop to help Group 2 in South Vaagso, and signalled back to his colonel that reinforcements were on their way. In the meantime, the rest of Group 3 would continue with the demolitions while half of Capt Ronald's troop was despatched across the Ulvesund to destroy the large herring oil factory at Mortenes.

Naval Actions in the Ulvesund

Back on HMS *Kenya*, Brig Haydon had been concerned that little had been heard from Group 3 on Maaloy, but recent news, at 0920hrs, that Churchill's group had taken the whole of the island meant that he could now safely commit his floating reserve to the main force in South Vaagso. After some difficulty, Durnford-Slater was raised on the radio and Haydon offered him help. The news that the Maaloy batteries had been captured and put out of action was passed on to R Adm Burrough. This was information he had been anxiously waiting for; the navy could now send destroyers through the narrow channel between Maaloy and Vaagso Island, the Maaloysund, into the Ulvesund and go looking for enemy ships to sink.

At 0930hrs, the destroyers *Oribi* and *Onslow* took up positions ready to enter Ulvesund, but found that the smoke was still too thick to pass through Maaloysund safely. Two minutes later, much to everyone's surprise, the single

As the ferocity of the fighting in South Vaagso continues, more and more men became casualties. Lt Denis O'Flaherty of No. 2 Troop is helped back to one of the landing craft for passage back to medical facilities onboard the warships. (IWM, N495)

gun remaining intact in the German battery at Rugsundo opened fire. The shells landed close to *Kenya*, which returned fire almost immediately with her 'A' and 'B' turrets. This return fire was too much for the enemy, and the crew of the coastal gun withdrew to their shelter for safety. Yet Burrough was not content for his ships to sit in full view of this troublesome battery. He ordered *Chiddingfold* to mask the warships from view of the Rugsundo battery by towing smoke floats across their line of fire and by making smoke from her funnel. Also included in the orders were instructions to 'move fast' in order not to be hit. This it did with alacrity, and also managed to get a few salvos of its own off towards the persistent gun before it moved away into the smoke screen.

At the same time, 0930hrs, the first of the Blenheim fighters arrived from their base in Scotland. It was intended that these fighters would be in radio contact with the floating headquarters on *Kenya*, but the radio-telephone link between ship and aircraft had failed. The plan was that the fighters would be directed by observers below, but this process did not materialize. The ships had sufficient anti-aircraft firepower to put up a considerable barrage against attacking enemy aircraft, providing that friendly aircraft had a controller looking after their interests from onboard the headquarters ship.

This failure in communications led to one fatal mishap, when the first of the enemy's fighters appeared over the area at 1005hrs. Two Me 109s came screaming in to engage the RAF aircraft. One of the Messerschmitts came in low underneath one of the Blenheims. It then pulled up and let loose a long

**27 DECEMBER
1941**

**0930hrs
Blenheim fighters
arrive over
Vaagso**

Once Maaloy Island had been completely cleared of the enemy, warships could move through the narrow strait between the island and South Vaagso. Here the destroyer HMS *Onslow* slips through the narrow stretch of water to engage enemy shipping in Ulvesund. (IWM, N521)

burst of fire into the RAF fighter's underside. The Blenheim's crew were oblivious to the German aircraft's presence, although all those watching from below could have given it sufficient warning if they were able. The Blenheim was fatally crippled by the fire and veered off and crashed into one of the mountains that overlooked the fjord, with the loss of all of its crew. As a later report explained: 'If efficient Radio/Telephone communication between ship and aircraft could have been established and maintained this Blenheim would possibly not have been lost.'

The two enemy Me 109s had arrived from Herdla airfield, the closest Luftwaffe base to Vaagso. They had been kept at operational readiness, with immediate notice to engage any British aircraft that entered the airspace assigned to the base, hence they were fuelled and ready to go when news of the British landings was received. There was a complete squadron of Me 109s at Herdla, but it would take time for them all to be de-iced and made ready for combat, so they would arrive later in the battle. The original plan for Operation *Archery* had called for the base at Herdla to be bombed by Stirlings earlier that morning in order to put it and the fighters out of action. Bomber Command, however, had cancelled this raid, and also the one that had been scheduled for Stavanger aerodrome. Herdla could now send its fighters to Vaagso, 30 minutes' flying time away, and it could also be used as a refuelling base for aircraft coming forward from Stavanger. Plans for Herdla to be attacked by Blenheims from 110 and 114 Squadrons were, however, still on schedule to take place at noon. Until then it would remain operational, with its fighters able to interfere with the landings.

Elsewhere, more Luftwaffe aircraft were also on the move. The landings on the Lofoten Islands on 26 December had prompted the enemy to despatch a number of its aircraft northwards against the concentration of British

Coastal Command bombers hit the Luftwaffe fighter base at Herdla just after midday. Bombs can be seen exploding on the runway and amongst the hangars and buildings of the airfield. (Author's collection)

warships gathered in the inland waterways of northern Norway. This decision was made before the landings at Vaagso had been reported. Intercepted signals showed that the Germans were diverting aircraft, including dive-bombers, from as far away as Denmark to Bodo airfield near Lofoten. Vaagso was under the flight path of these aircraft, which did not bode well for those engaged in Operation *Archery*. It was imperative that the intended bombing of Herdla airfield take place later that morning in order to deny the use of the aerodrome as a refuelling base to those German aircraft in transit.

The smoke screen that had covered the landing points was, at around 0945hrs, clearing sufficiently to allow the destroyers *Oribi* and *Onslow* to move through the narrow waterway of Maaloysund to enter Ulvesund. On board *Oribi* was Capt Birney's Group 5 with the half troop of men from 2 Commando. Its task was to land north of the town and set up a roadblock to protect the northern flank of the landings, stopping the enemy advancing towards South Vaagso from that direction. It was also to send a fighting patrol into the smaller village of North Vaagso and destroy any German presence there.

The two warships slowly crept through the channel with *Oribi* in the lead, passing near South Vaagso. The sudden appearance of destroyers close to the fighting in the town switched German attention momentarily eastwards. The enemy troops who had up until then been resisting British troop movements through the town, now turned their guns on the huge targets that were sliding slowly by just a few hundred yards away. They peppered the warships with a welter of small-arms fire, taking pot shots at anyone on board who showed themselves. Three of *Oribi*'s crew were wounded.

Once the destroyers had cleared the smoke and fire in the narrow confines of Maaloysund, the wider waters of Ulvesund were opened up before them. The long fjord, flanked by high snow-covered mountains, made an impressive sight, but there were also more pleasing objects closer to hand. Ahead of them were tempting maritime targets. The armed trawler *Föhn*, two Norwegian steamers – the *Normar* and the *Remar Edzard Fritzen* – and one Dutch steamer, the *Eismeer*, all of which had been commandeered by the Germans, had been frantically trying to get up enough steam to break out to the north and were now slowly underway. The British destroyers arrived at an opportune moment; a few minutes later and the enemy ships would have been well underway.

The master of the *Föhn*, Leutnant zur See Lohr, immediately gave orders to engage the two destroyers with the ship's twin Oerlikon anti-aircraft guns, in a brave attempt to slow them down. The odds were against achieving anything more than a show of defiance, but the German crew stuck resolutely to their task and light 20mm shells began splattering the superstructure of the *Onslow*, which was closing quickly on the German trawler. Lohr then gave instructions for the three merchant vessels to beach themselves and he swung his ship to port and rammed the shore at full speed. *Onslow* returned fire, from which the *Föhn*'s master was killed along with several of his men. The remainder of the crew scrambled ashore and

▽ EVENTS

1 0739hrs – Operation *Archery*'s attack force makes contact with the submarine *Tuna* and prepares to enter Vaagsfjord.

2 The flotilla passes the German look out post on Husevaag Island just as Hampden bombers fly low overhead and attack the German coast defence guns on Rugsundo.

3 HMS *Kenya* and the destroyers arrive at their bombarding positions opposite Vaagso Island.

4 The two troop transports, *Prince Charles* and *Prince Leopold* move into the tiny bay opposite Hollevik to disembark the commandos.

5 0842hrs – The commando groups leave their transport ships and head towards the landing beaches.

6 0848hrs – *Kenya* and the destroyers open fire on the German battery on Maaloy Island.

7 0856hrs – Rugsundo Battery opens fire on *Kenya* but is silenced by return fire.

8 0859hrs – Hampden aircraft lay smoke over landing beaches at South Vaagso and Maaloy Island and the commando attack begins.

9 0932hrs – Rugsundo Battery opens fire on HMS *Kenya* again and is once more silenced by return fire.

10 0940hrs – HMS *Chiddingfold* lays smoke to hide the warships from the Rugsundo Battery.

11 0945hrs – HMS *Oribi* and *Onslow* enter Ulvesund through the straits of Maaloysund.

12 0950hrs – *Oribi* and *Onslow* engage German shipping in Ulvesund. *Onslow* destroys three enemy steamers, the *Eisner*, the *Norma* and the *Fritzen* and the armed trawler *Föhn*.

13 1020hrs – Group 5 commandos are landed near North Vaagso.

14 During the morning two other enemy vessels, the steamship *Anita L. M. Russ* and an armoured tug, the *Rechtenfleth*, enter Ulvesund from the north and are put out of action by the destroyers.

15 1200hrs – The commandos of Group 5 are evacuated after completing their tasks and the destroyers move down Ulvesund to rejoin the ships in Vaagsfjord.

16 1210hrs – The German armed trawler *Donne* and the steamship *Anhalt* are intercepted and dealt with at the entrance to Vaagsfjord by the destroyer HMS *Offa*.

17 1217hrs – South Vaagso has been cleared of enemy troops for demolition work to begin.

18 1310hrs – Troops begin withdrawing from South Vaagso.

19 1317hrs – HMS *Kenya* is hit by a shell fired by Rugsundo Battery. The cruiser again returns fire and the German position is finally put out of action.

20 1434hrs – re-embarkation is complete and ships make ready to sail.

21 1500hrs – the ships of Operation *Archery* clear Vaagsfjord and set course for Scapa Flow.

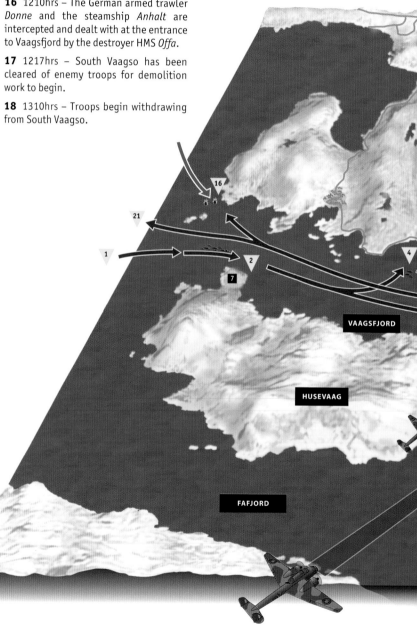

OPERATION *ARCHERY*: THE RAID ON VAAGSO

27 DECEMBER 1941

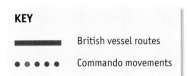

KEY

━━━━━━ British vessel routes

• • • • • Commando movements

MAIN OBJECTIVES AND GERMAN DEFENCES **1 – 7**

1 Group 1 landings
2 Group 2 landings
3 Group 3 landings
4 Group 5 landings
5 Maaloy coast defence battery
6 Rugsundo coast defence battery
7 Husevaag lookout

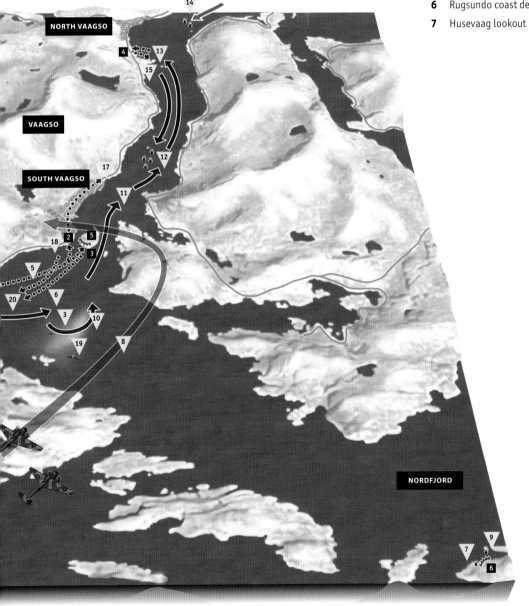

NORTH VAAGSO

VAAGSO

SOUTH VAAGSO

NORDFJORD

continued their defiant stand with the small arms they carried. This fire was only silenced when *Onslow* fired its main weapons against them – a sledgehammer to crack a nut. Unable to compete with this show of strength, the survivors made off inland. A short distance away, the *Normar* and the *Remar Edzard Fritzen* were both beached successfully. The *Onslow* put boarding parties aboard the two Norwegian vessels. The *Eismeer* remained stationary out in the fjord, unable to generate enough steam to get underway before the action started. It was later sunk by shell fire from the warships.

Whilst *Onslow* was engaged in its little sea battle, *Oribi* steamed on up the Ulvesund to disembark Capt Birney's Group 5 on Vaagso Island north of the main town. At 1020hrs the group was landed just south of the village of North Vaagso. They went ashore unopposed and immediately set about blocking the road that ran alongside the Ulvesund. A fighting patrol then moved up the road into North Vaagso and was able to capture a number of prisoners, including some of the German seamen who had escaped from the beached ships and the most prominent collaborator in the village. The commandos then searched the buildings for enemy papers and took over the telephone and telegraph office.

Out on the Ulvesund, there was more action taking place, for two enemy ships came sailing down the inland waterway oblivious to the battle that was raging ahead of them. In the lead was an armoured tug, the *Rechtenfleth*, followed by the German merchant ship the *Anita L.M. Russ*. Both vessels realized their mistake too late and, just as the British warships began to open

Reinforcements from Capt Peter Young's No. 6 Troop are ferried over from Maaloy to help with the street fighting in South Vaagso. (IWM, N479)

fire, they swung violently for shore to beach themselves. Both were destroyed by naval gunfire from the two destroyers. The day had been an effective one for the British warships, for five enemy vessels, amounting to more than 15,000 tons, had been sunk or put out of action.

Capt Birney and his group of men from 2 Commando had meanwhile blown up the telephone and telegraph post in North Vaagso and withdrawn back down the road. A short time later they were fired on by German troops moving out of the village behind them. The commander of the German gun battery at Halsoer, Leutnant Lienkamp, had sent a platoon of infantry southwards to find out what was happening in South Vaagso. An advance party of these troops now made contact with Birney's outpost guarding the road. After a short firefight in which one of the Germans was killed, the enemy retreated back to North Vaagso. A short while later the Germans tried again, this time with the whole platoon. Thus far Birney's group had taken no casualties and it seemed pointless for him to hold on for too long in such an exposed position. The captain decided it was time to withdraw, as he had achieved all of his original objectives. He gave orders to blow a large crater in the road and then signalled to the *Oribi* to come and pick up his group.

It only took minutes for the *Oribi* to arrive back on the scene and allow Group 5 to return to the destroyer. The withdrawal prompted the enemy to press forward and to rake the retreating commandos with small-arms fire. Fortunately, the nearby destroyer had bigger guns to counter this fire, and sent the enemy ducking for cover. The shoreline and road were sprayed with rounds from various calibres of automatic weapons and cannons. *Onslow* also came close and hosed the area with even more fire in order to cover the commandos' escape route back to the *Oribi*. It took only a short while for the raiding party to return onboard the *Oribi* and for the small boats to be lifted and stowed. Once everything was secure, the two destroyers swung around to the south, heading back towards the battle which was still being fought in the streets of South Vaagso.

Consolidation in South Vaagso

Back on Maaloy, Capt Young's No. 6 Troop was mopping up the remnants of German resistance and trying to winkle out individual enemy soldiers from their hiding places. Young reported to Maj Churchill at his headquarters on the beach at around 1015hrs, explaining that the major part of his tasks had been completed. It was now the turn of the demolition parties to complete their work. Churchill told the captain that the rest of 3 Commando was having trouble clearing South Vaagso and that LtCol Durnford-Slater wished him to send reinforcements. The major ordered Young to take half of his troop across the Maaloysund to help with the street fighting in the town.

When Young arrived in South Vaagso with his men, he was given a situation report by the colonel. He was told that only one officer remained unscathed in the two troops that had been attacking through the town. Both troop commanders and Capt Linge had been killed. Durnford-Slater then explained how he was going to get things moving again. He intended to put more troops

Bright sunshine lights the scene during a pause in the fighting in South Vaagso as more wounded are brought out of the battle. (IWM, N456)

into the attack. The floating reserve would be arriving shortly at his headquarters. Lt Clements' Group 1 party from No. 2 Troop had just come up the road from Hollevik to join in and Capt Bradley was trying to spare as many of his men as possible from the demolition tasks allocated to his No. 1 Troop. All of these commandos would now be put into the attack to sweep through the centre and north of the town as quickly as possible. He wanted Young to move through and clear the buildings on the right along the waterfront, whilst the new reinforcements attacked through the middle of the town.

Since arriving in the town, Young noticed that there appeared to be little movement being made by the troops he had seen. Most seemed to have stopped and were huddled by the sides of the buildings looking around corners. Rapid movement was desperately needed to put pressure on the enemy. Fortunately there was more firepower in the town now, more guns and rifles to ensure that the enemy kept their heads down. Young took his half-troop into the buildings close to the water and leapfrogged their way forward. His men worked in harmony – whilst a few kept up a steady fire into windows and doorways, others would scoot across roads and open spaces. Commandos would pour into a house or factory through the doorway, run through the building and out the back, whilst those outside kept the enemy snipers occupied. If any of the enemy inside failed to be located or refused to come out, the building was set on fire.

More men were attacking now on a much wider front, all pressing forward and leaving the enemy with no time to organize a new defensive line. The amount of fire being poured into buildings was immense. The barrage was supplemented by the guns of the two destroyers stationed in the Maaloysund. Progress through the town by the commandos was monitored by the ships' crews, and whenever the enemy was identified their guns would open fire with rounds much heavier than those available to those troops fighting on shore. The balance of power began to shift positively in favour of Durnford-Slater's men. There were still more casualties to be taken before the day was out, but the battle for possession of the town was gradually being won by the commandos.

During the advance, the colonel came up to join Young's party in a tiny woodyard. It was an inopportune moment, for the captain's whole group were stuck fast, unable to move because of a sniper. The enemy marksman had already shot two of Young's men and was sure to kill more – every time someone tried to move, the sniper would fire. He was pinpointed to an upper floor in a house behind them. When a third man was shot, Young knew something positive had to be done. In a shed close by, a can of petrol was found. Young gave orders for Sgt Herbert to take the petrol and throw it into the house when he gave the signal. He then shouted for everyone to stand up and fire into the windows of the building. Under the covering fire, Herbert raced across to the house and tossed the petrol inside, lobbing a grenade in after it. Within seconds there was an explosion, followed by a sheet of flame. The building soon became a raging inferno that engulfed the whole house, along with the enemy sniper inside.

There were no more serious incidents such as this as the commandos pressed their way through the town. One group located the enemy tank that was known to be in South Vaagso. The obsolete pre-war light tank was located in a shed, and steps were immediately taken to demolish it. Demolitions officers placed charges and lit the fuses. Unfortunately, too much explosive was used and one of the demolition party was killed and another injured by the blast when the charge was fired.

German prisoners are escorted to the rear on their way into captivity back in England. These smartly turned out individuals are most likely headquarters staff who gave up the fight when confronted with determined commandos. (IWM, N451)

Fighting in South Vaagso has here reached the northern end of the town. All German opposition has been eliminated and the commandos prepare to hold the outskirts of the built-up area against any possible enemy counter-attack. The time is drawing near for the withdrawal to begin. (IWM, N487)

By late morning, Young's men had reached the far end of the town and set up a position in a solidly built house by the side of the main road. Durnford-Slater once again came forward to assess the situation. The colonel had been everywhere that morning, moving from troop to troop, always in the open and always amongst the worst of the fighting. At one point, a grenade had exploded close by, throwing him through the air. The two orderlies alongside him were seriously wounded, but the colonel escaped with just a few scratches. Durnford-Slater told Young to hold his outpost until at least 1310hrs and then gradually withdraw back to the main landing area. The advance had reached its high point and the demolition teams now had to complete their work before the evacuation could start. The colonel reported back to force headquarters at 1230hrs, stating that after personally directing operations in the town he was convinced that enemy resistance had been largely overcome and that demolitions were in progress.

Air and Naval Battles around Vaagsfjord

Above the street fighting in South Vaagso that morning, sharp actions were also being fought by aircraft. The enemy put in a number of appearances, usually with just two or three Me 109s or a couple of He 111s at any one time. Many of the enemy planes were chased off by concentrated anti-aircraft fire from the ships, or by the intervention of the fighters. The Allied aircraft began to arrive at 0930hrs and they carried on flying operations throughout the day until 1615hrs.

Just after 1236hrs, a more concentrated enemy raid took place, with waves of He 111 bombers attacking over the Vaagsfjord. Each formation, however, contained just three bombers and each was given a hostile reception by the ships' guns. All the Heinkels dropped their bombs wide of the mark and no ships suffered any damage.

There was, however, some damage done to one of the warships at 1300hrs, when *Kenya* once again came under fire from the troublesome

Rugsundo battery. The first round missed and the cruiser was quick to reply in kind with its main guns in 'X' and 'Y' turrets at the rear of the ship, and with its 4in secondary guns. Undaunted, the Germans fired again. The next shell from Rugsundo hit the *Kenya* on its armoured belt and a few minutes later the cruiser suffered a near miss abreast of the port torpedo tubes. A shell splinter injured one of its ratings. The warship kept firing, whilst the coastal battery's crew this time seemed determined to stick to their gun. At 1317hrs, another shell hit the *Kenya*, creating a hole in the ship about 10ft above the waterline abreast of the bridge. By this time, *Kenya*'s gunners were getting truly aggravated by the problematic enemy battery and poured concentrated fire onto it. A few minutes later it fell silent, never to burst into life again.

Just before midday at Herdla, 80 miles to the south of Vaagso, enemy air raid sirens wailed to signal an incoming air attack. Thirteen Blenheim bombers from Coastal Command 114 Squadron, each carrying four 250lb bombs and a number of 4lb incendiaries, swept down over the German airfield. Each of them lined up their attack run with the wooden runway and braved the sporadic flak that came up to meet them. At 1202hrs, flying at just 250ft, the bombers came in one after another to drop their high-explosive bombs neatly on the runway laid out before them. The small incendiaries tumbled from the aircraft, scattering themselves amongst the wooden huts and buildings. Then, its task completed, each aircraft rose up swiftly and leaned into a sharp turn to speed away. One unfortunate aircraft suffered a direct hit from an 88mm anti-aircraft shell and burst into flames. The Blenheim then swerved violently colliding with another and both crashed into the sea. The remainder continued up into cloud and were gone, winging their way back to the safety of their Scottish airfields. Behind them the

Assault landing craft wait as more of the wounded are returned to the boats. (IWM, N481)

27 DECEMBER 1941

1236hrs
He 111 bombers attack the Allied ships

mangled wooden runway was littered with debris and cratered by 20 direct hits. The huts on the perimeter were all engulfed by fire. The RAF had rendered Herdla aerodrome no longer serviceable to enemy aircraft.

Earlier that morning, whilst the landings were in progress, the destroyer HMS *Offa* was given the task of protecting the naval force from the west by guarding the entrance to Vaagsfjord. The morning had been quiet, other than some attention from a few enemy aircraft, which were driven off by anti-aircraft fire. Shortly after noon, two German ships turned into the fjord from the north. They had approached the inland waterway unaware of the fact that a battle was in progress half way along it. Noise from the fighting was hidden from the two ships by the high mountains in the centre of Vaagso Island. Once they entered the fjord it was too late, for the *Offa* immediately spotted them, reported their presence to Burrough's headquarters and began closing rapidly on the two vessels. *Chiddingfold* was then ordered to move down the fjord to support *Offa*.

The first of the enemy ships was an armed trawler, the *Donner*; the second a merchant steamer, the *Anhalt*. The steamer immediately put her rudder hard to port, increased speed and ran for the shore, beaching herself securely in shallow water before either of the two destroyers could interfere. *Chiddingfold* closed on the stranded ship just as her crew had taken to their boats. They pulled to shore with all speed and ignored *Chiddingfold*'s requests for them to heave to. The captain on the destroyer's bridge advised the oarsmen by loud hailer that he would open fire if they did not halt, but

The withdrawal begins and the men of 3 Commando slowly make their way back to the boats. Demolition work on targets close to the embarkation point is now implemented. (IWM, N516)

again they spurned the warning and continued pulling for shore. The first shell from the destroyer sank one of the boats. The other, although hit, succeeded in escaping to the shore, for the *Chiddingfold*'s attention was forced skywards when the heaviest of the enemy air raids began.

The armed trawler had meanwhile managed to turn to starboard and head for the open sea, making a speed of 10 knots. It was a pointless flight, however, for the *Offa* was capable of three times that speed, and she gradually began to overrun the small vessel. The captain ordered a warning shot to be fired whilst blinking out a message to the *Donner* to stop. When it was clear that the trawler intended to try to escape, the destroyer fired again and scored several hits. The *Offa* then came alongside the vessel and boarded her. The crew was captured and the boat taken as a prize. It was the intention to put a crew aboard the trawler and to steam her back to Scotland. Unfortunately, she had insufficient fuel for the journey, and the trawler was sunk instead.

German Shipping Sunk During Operation *Archery*

Vessel	Tonnage
Föhn (armed trawler)	250 tons
SS *Remar Edzard Fritzen*	3,000 tons
SS *Normar* ex *Calypso*	2,200 tons
Rechtenfleth (armed tug)	200 tons
SS *Anita L.M. Russ*	2,800 tons
SS *Eismeer*	1,000 tons
SS *Anhalt*	5,930 tons
Donner (armed trawler)	250 tons
Total tonnage destroyed	15,630 tons

Withdrawal and Evacuation

Back in South Vaagso, demolition work was being carried out by groups of specialist soldiers. Some of the enemy-occupied buildings were put to the torch, whilst others were demolished with high explosives. Most of the explosives brought ashore for the task were put to good use: 300lb of plastic explosive; 1,100lb of guncotton; 150lb of ammonal; 150 incendiary bombs; 60 guncotton primers and 1,400ft of fuse. One particular industrial plant was too close to the embarkation point chosen for the evacuation, so it was decided that this factory would be the last to be blown.

With enemy resistance over and the roads into the town guarded, Durnford-Slater could start the evacuation and begin sending troops back to the transport ships. There had been a ferry service out to the ships in the fjord running all day, carrying casualties back for medical help and returning with reinforcements and supplies. Now the boats were given over to the process of bringing out the raiding force. Durnford-Slater had planned for an orderly withdrawal, starting with troops nearest to the jetties where the assault craft would land. One troop would hold the area surrounding this point and would

OVERLEAF: Operation *Archery* was very much a combined effort with each of the services playing their part. While the RAF kept the skies clear, the Royal Navy took the commandos ashore and brought them back again. Each commando knew that at the end of the operation, or if he was wounded, he would never be left behind as a prisoner. All day long the small landing craft ploughed their way back and forth to their mother ships ferrying men, arms and ammunition ashore, and bringing back wounded soldiers, German prisoners and Norwegian volunteers. When the raid was over the boats were still there at hand ready to bring the last man out.

be last to leave. When the bulk of troops in the town had got away, those holding the outskirts would be called in. After they had left, the last factory would be blown and the rear party would leave. At 1245hrs the colonel gave the order for the withdrawal to begin, first with No. 2 Troop along with those survivors of No. 4 Troop, then No. 6 Troop and finally No. 1 Troop.

On the extreme northern edge of the lodgement, Capt Young had noticed things had settled down somewhat: 'It had become as quiet as a grave,' he noted later. He noticed that there was no sign of either side at his end of the town. It was now 1300hrs and he decided it was time to pull out. The captain sent the bulk of his men back to the boats and then followed with a small rearguard. Their route through the town was punctuated by burning buildings and littered with dead Germans. Young counted 15 enemy dead lying in the open, although most of the German casualties had been inside buildings.

At the embarkation point, most of the troops had been evacuated by the time Young arrived. It just remained for 3 Commando's rearguard to set off and the nearby factory to be blown. After Young and his men left the shore, the order was given for the last fish oil production site to be razed to the ground. The three-minute fuse was set by Sgt Millar and everyone sought cover as he made his hurried exit from the building, blowing a warning whistle. This final act of destruction culminated in a huge explosion that

The remains of a Norwegian oil factory are spread across the waterside after it had been blown to bits by explosives. (IWM, N491)

shook the earth, and the factory burst apart in sheets of flame and billowing smoke. At 1408hrs, the colonel radioed back to Force Headquarters that all troops had left the shore and all demolitions were complete. It was the end of the military operation. The final landing craft gradually filled with the remaining troops of the rearguard and then, the last man ashore, LtCol Durnford-Slater, stepped onboard to give the order to cast off. By 1434hrs, all landing craft had been hoisted onto the assault ships and the flotilla was ready to sail.

By this time, all the other ships had also prepared themselves for sea and R Adm Burrough gave the signal for the destroyers to move down the fjord to form a screen for the assault ships and the *Kenya*. As they passed the beached *Anhalt*, the *Oribi* and the *Onslow* gave the stricken vessel a few parting shots from their main armament. HMS *Kenya* did the same when she came abreast of the steamship, although the cruiser did a much more thorough job, for she hove to and pumped 15 6in shells into the enemy ship at almost point blank range, leaving it a burning wreck.

It was almost dark when the fleet of ships reached the open sea at around 1500hrs. They had just cleared the fjord when the Luftwaffe put in its last appearance. A formation of Heinkel bombers came over intent on making an attack before the night closed in. All of the warships opened up on the

Commandos on the hills above South Vaagso look down on the continuing destruction that is being meted out to the town. (IWM, N478)

27 DECEMBER 1941

1245hrs Withdrawal from South Vaagso commences

27 DECEMBER 1941

1408hrs Withdrawal from South Vaagso complete

enemy aircraft with a great variety of guns, filling the sky with tracers and explosions. The concentration of fire was too much for the enemy pilots and none were able to close onto their targets; all of them dropped their sticks of bombs well wide of the mark. Then they were gone, leaving the raiding force to continue its journey home unmolested.

Once darkness had fallen completely, a large alteration of course was made to fool the enemy. Aboard the now-quiet ships, the commandos and crews of the landing craft were able to grab a few moments of well-deserved rest, whilst the navy plotted their route to Scapa Flow and safety. On board his flagship, R Adm Burrough signalled the Admiralty in London with news of the completion of the raid, and confirmed that Operation *Archery* had been a complete success.

At 1600hrs on 28 December, the raiders steamed into the great naval anchorage to congratulations from everyone there, including the press. Admiral Burrough's signal had prompted the Admiralty to release news of the operation and the whole world was eager for the full story. The success of the raid was exploited and described in detail, as far as security would allow, to the people of Britain and the Commonwealth, all of whom were hungry for good news. The war was by then more than two years old, and the nation was desperate for some sign that the country was fighting back. Inflicting a bloody nose on the enemy in his own backyard was just what the people wanted to hear.

For many, however, the raid had mortal consequences. It was the first real test for the commando organization, the first time its men had fought face-to-face with the enemy in prolonged action, and inevitably there were casualties. During the raid, the commandos lost 2 officers and 15 other ranks killed, with 5 officers and 48 other ranks wounded. The Norwegian party lost just one officer killed, the brave Capt Linge. The navy also suffered losses, with two ratings killed and two officers and four ratings injured. Eight aircraft were missing whilst supporting the raid.

ANALYSIS

On the night of 27 December 1941, as R Adm Burrough's triumphant force made its way back to the safety of Scapa Flow, R Adm Hamilton was having some misgivings regarding events that had taken place earlier that day. Much further to the north, he had brought Force 'J' into Vestfjord on 26 December and dispersed his ships amongst the Lofoten Islands completely according to plan. Sweeps by his destroyers had been made amongst the surrounding waterways; two Norwegian steamships had been captured, an armed German trawler had been sunk, 12 Commando had landed without casualties and a small number of enemy soldiers had been rounded up. Then

The last of the raiders return to the boats for embarkation. The raid is over, the town and its factories have been destroyed, it is time to go home. (IWM, N522)

an enemy reconnaissance plane flew round and round the anchorage, no doubt reporting to its base the presence of the British flotilla. On the 27th it was back again, followed a little later by a lone Heinkel He 115, which came in low and dropped a single bomb perilously close to Hamilton's headquarters ship HMS *Arethusa*. The cruiser was shaken, but undamaged.

Hamilton felt this was a precursor of things to come, and reported the matter to C-in-C Home Fleet, Adm Tovey, back at Scapa Flow. Earlier that day, the Admiralty had informed Hamilton that 30 Junkers Ju 88 and nine He 111 aircraft had arrived at Stavanger, and a further nine Ju 87s were due at Bodo on the 28th. More aircraft were also being moved from eastern France to Norway. The Germans were massing their aircraft for the attack. At 2256hrs, Tovey sent a signal to Hamilton instructing him not to hesitate to withdraw if he considered the air threat serious.

By 1124hrs the next morning, Hamilton had decided that the enemy moves were a serious threat to his fleet of ships. He was anxious that they were confined to inshore waters with a large number of enemy bombers on their way. He gave orders for Force 'J' to sail for home that night. The single bomb that had landed close to *Arethusa* was enough to convince him that all of his vessels were at great risk. Operation *Anklet* was over. It did not last the three weeks that were planned, instead just a little over two days. Its prize was one small enemy craft sunk, two Norwegian steamships disabled, 29 prisoners taken, two quislings removed and 299 Norwegian refugees brought back to Britain. It was not the sort of achievement that had been envisaged when the 22 vessels set out six days before.

The landing craft that pull away from South Vaagso leave a trail of destruction behind them. Buildings burn and dead Germans litter the streets, and billowing clouds of black smoke indicate the work of the commandos. (IWM, 529)

When Churchill heard of the outcome of the operation he was, quite rightly, most displeased. His rage was summed up in a very confidential minute sent to the Chiefs of Staff Committee carrying the security heading 'HUSH – MOST SECRET' in large red letters:

> If the fact that the enemy assembled a certain number of aircraft within striking distance of ANKLET was to be held a good reason for an immediate retreat this operation should never have been undertaken. It was always understood that we should be attacked from the air, whether we occupied Bodo or the ANKLET islands. The proposal of the ANKLET islands was based upon adequate antiaircraft artillery being mounted afloat or ashore, and the configuration of the fjord affording the necessary protection. Moreover, the object was the interruption over an indefinite period of the German north and south traffic in iron ore and supplies against Russia. The ANKLET episode must, therefore, be judged a marked failure, as it was abandoned hastily and without any facts being apparent which had not been foreseen at the time of its inception and preparation.

The same reaction was not given to Operation *Archery*. The raid on Vaagso was deemed to be a complete success and its list of achievements was long. The raiders and their supporting forces had completed all their tasks, which included: the destruction of all targeted coastal defence guns, German barracks, headquarters and administration buildings; the elimination of all enemy troops in the area; the demolition of all known fish oil and canning plants; and the sabotage of the enemy infrastructure, such as telephone cables, petrol stores, ammunition dumps, searchlights and lighthouses. In addition, the commandos had fought and gained the upper hand over the enemy and learned much in the process. They had gained combat experience in amphibious landings, street fighting and demolition missions, and completed them according to plan. The Royal Navy had transported the assault force exactly on time to their desired destination, kept it secure from surface attack and returned it safely to its home port. The RAF had dominated the skies over the target and dealt with all interference from enemy aircraft.

Back in Vaagso, on 28 December the Germans were trying to sort out what had taken place. The British had left no man as prisoner of war, for all the wounded had been evacuated. There were few of the Germans left to tale the tale either, for those captured included the wounded, who had been taken back to Britain. All that remained were the bodies. The commanding general of the 181st Division, Kurt Woytasch, visited the scene and was confronted with devastation. On Maaloy Island there was not one German to be found. There were 11 German bodies left and 35 men were missing.

It was clear that the area had been subjected to a well-planned and well-executed raid. It also seemed that the raiders had sufficiently good intelligence to know exactly what to expect, where to go and what to attack. They had singled out every defensive position and every gun battery. They seemed to know the strength of the garrison and the location of likely reinforcements. The immediate thought was that there was a Norwegian

German prisoners line up along the decks of HMS *Prince Leopold* after their capture during the raid. (IWM, N454)

resistance cell on Vaagso in contact with the British – the Germans took subsequent steps to find it. And then there was the question of just how much help and support the local civilians gave to the invaders? The area was put under immediate curfew and each house thoroughly searched. There was a clampdown on all movement and life was made miserable for the inhabitants for a while, but there was little direct retaliation by the Germans. A few people were rounded up and taken to concentration camps, but most continued with their lives as before. Fortunately, although several civilians were wounded during the short battle through the streets, only one Norwegian lost his life – it was thought that he was killed by a stray piece of shrapnel.

In London, some friction arose between the Norwegian government-in-exile and the British government. The Norwegians were unhappy they had not been told of the details of Operation *Archery* prior to the raid. It was British policy not to divulge the target of an intended raid to any outside agency for fear of breaches of security. There was always a problem with exiled governments regarding attacks on their homeland. Understandably, they wished to be consulted about any raid that might harm their citizens and they were always fearful of German reprisals. In this particular case, the Free Norwegians felt that such raids were mere pinpricks, with little strategic value. They served merely to raise false hopes and invite enemy retribution. Operation *Anklet* was a case in point. When the troops landed in the Lofotens, they convinced the local Norwegians that they had arrived for a considerable stay. Many gave them great assistance only to be told after two days that the British were pulling out. Those who had supported and helped the troops were given the option of leaving with the commandos or staying to face the Germans when they retook the area. This virtually amounted to a choice between deportation or retribution.

There were recriminations elsewhere amongst the German hierarchy in Norway. Intelligence reports received via Sweden claimed that there was a furious exchange of telegrams between Oslo and Berlin regarding the British raids. Generaloberst von Falkenhorst, General Officer Commanding Norway, accused German Coastal Battery Command of gross neglect of duty. He issued a reprimand and notified that in future it would be taken under his direct personal control. Coastal Battery Command baulked at this snub and appealed to Berlin against the ruling and against the reprimand. The same intelligence source also noted that Norwegian High Command reported to Berlin that British naval actions off the coast of Norway were causing grave anxiety. The authorities were concerned about the viability of maintaining Norwegian coastal traffic and lamented the loss of two vessels, which had been sunk during the raid, carrying large stocks of ammunition for the coastal batteries. Ammunition reserves, they noted, were dangerously low.

Another secret telegram sent to the Foreign Office in London from Stockholm spoke of German reaction to the Vaagso raid in particular:

> The raiders have caused bickerings amongst commanders and that fresh dispositions of occupying troops are being made and garrisons increased. Raids are being regarded by the Germans as being practice raids rather than preludes to a serious invasion. News of the Maaloy raid caused a stampede amongst garrisons, many soldiers running away and hiding in the mountains and leaving garages open and electric lights burning.

To Hitler the raids reinforced a belief he had long held that Norway was the zone of destiny in the war. Churchill also shared this preoccupation, and had instructed his Chiefs of Staff in 1941 to draw up plans for an invasion. The CIGS (from December 1941), Gen Alan Brooke, had always been horrified by this suggestion, realizing that the logistical problems in mounting such an invasion, even with American help, would be beyond their present capabilities. Certainly there were sound reasons for believing that Norway could be a base from which, as Churchill put it, 'to unroll the map of Europe from the North', but most military minds thought that such a move would place their forces in a strategic backwater. Hitler knew the immense value that Norway brought to his war effort through the country's rich natural resources. Gen Falkenhorst's plea for more men to guard the coastline was heeded by Hitler, and an immediate reinforcement of 12,000 men was despatched to the country. A further 18,000 followed within months to help establish a network of fortress and coastal defence battalions. The Nazi dictator also told the head of the Kriegsmarine,

28 DECEMBER 1941

1600hrs Raiding force enters Scapa Flow

Jubilant commandos and Norwegian civilians pose for the cameraman after the raid. The refugees are fleeing Nazi tyranny hoping for a better life in Britain and to carry on the cause of liberating their country. (IWM, N474)

Admiral Erich Raeder, that he wished for all of Germany's capital ships to be based in Norway to help protect the sea routes along the coast and to interfere with Russian convoys. Over the remaining course of the war, more and more of Germany's strength was taken up occupying Norway. By the middle of 1944, the German garrison in Norway amounted to more than 350,000 troops, all of whom could have been better employed countering the Allied invasion of France or dealing with the Red Army, which was closing inexorably on the mother country.

CONCLUSION

Operation *Archery* was the first great raid carried out by the British during the war. The raids carried out by Combined Operations that had gone before had either been hit-and-run attacks or had been unopposed landings in quiet backwaters. At Vaagso, the commandos fought a major running battle with some very good German troops. The experiences gained there were passed on through instruction and training to future commandos. Those men who had taken part went on to employ their skills in other raids and landings in North Africa, Sicily and Italy.

Following the Vaagso action, Mountbatten and his team compiled other larger, more penetrative raids. At St Nazaire in March the following year, 2 Commando, with Royal Navy support, sailed up the River Loire, through German coastal defences, blew up the massive dry dock (using a Royal Navy destroyer packed with explosives) and destroyed dockyard facilities in the town. The RAF attempted to divert attention through prolonged operations overhead. The combined operation was termed 'the greatest raid of all' (see

After food, rest and a good wash, survivors of the raid pose for the cameraman during the voyage home. They felt, with good cause, that they had achieved a remarkable victory. (IWM, N511)

Osprey Campaign 92). Five months later, in August, an amphibious raid on a scale that resembled a mini invasion was launched against Dieppe (Osprey Campaign 127). The main body of troops were Canadian, but the commandos who landed on the flanks to attack coastal batteries included veterans of Vaagso. Unfortunately the raid was not a success, but the reasons for its failure helped focus the minds of the commanders on what was required to get troops ashore when the time came for the big invasion of Nazi-held Europe.

There was never another Allied raid of any notable size carried out on Norway. Intelligence-gathering landings were made and several airborne operations were launched by SOE saboteurs and British paratroopers on the heavy water plant at Vemork and the power station at Telemark, but no further large-scale landings were conducted. Norway was eventually liberated in 1945 at the war's end, when the German army of occupation laid down its arms without a struggle.

The raid on Vaagso demonstrated that the era of combined operations had truly arrived. Operation *Archery* involved all three services together right from the moment of its conception. Each of them provided a staff of planners to work closely together to integrate each other's tasks; preparations were made with due regard to the impact on other disciplines. In warfare, full-scale exercises are used to test plans and procedures in order to throw up problems that might be experienced during an operation. These also help to hone the skills needed for combat. Nothing can replace the actual experience of battle, however. Operation *Archery* gave everyone involved the opportunity to test the theories of combined operations and formulate processes that later became the yardsticks for future attacks. Amphibious warfare under the protective umbrella of air cover was the means by which the Allies were to return to the continent of Europe when the time came. The Vaagso raid was one of the small steps taken towards that goal.

The lessons learned from Operation *Archery* and other amphibious landings helped to train future soldiers over the next two years, so that when the British came to land in force on German-occupied Europe in the greatest invasion in history, on 6 June 1944, they were well prepared for the task. (battlefieldhistorian.com)

BIBLIOGRAPHY AND FURTHER READING

Books

Anon, *Supplement to the London Gazette of Friday 2nd July*, 1948, HMSO, London (1948)

Buckley, Christopher, *Norway, The Commandos, Dieppe*, HMSO, London (1951)

Devins, Joseph H., *The Vaagso Raid*, Robert Hale, London (1967)

Durnford-Slater, Brig John, *Commando*, William Kimber, London (1953)

St George Saunders, Hilary, *The Green Beret*, Michael Joseph, London (1949)

Young, LtCol Peter, *Storm from the Sea*, William Kimber, London (1958)

Files from the National Archives, Kew, London

ADM 1/20025	Despatch of report on the Vaagso Raid
ADM 116/4381	Operation Anklet
AIR 20/1050	Operation Archery
CAB 121/445	Operation Anklet
HS 2/226	Operation Archery
WO 106/1988	Report on Operation Anklet: Planning
WO 231/5	Operation Archery Raid on Vaagso Island
WO 199/3057	Operation Archery

INDEX

References to illustrations are shown in **bold**.